W9-DEV-195

the creative office

GingKo
PRESS

the creative office

Jeremy Myerson and Philip Ross

Published in 2002 by Gingko Press Inc.
5768 Paradise Drive, Suite J
Corte Madera, CA 94925
Phone (415) 924-9615
Fax (415) 924-9608
books@gingkopress.com
http://www.gingkopress.com

Published by arrangement with Laurence King Publishing

Copyright © 1999 Laurence King Publishing Ltd
This book was designed and produced by Laurence King Publishing Ltd,
London

All rights reserved. No part of this publication may be reproduced or
transmitted in any form or by any means, electronic or mechanical,
including photocopy, recording or any information storage and retrieval
system, without permission in writing from the publisher.

ISBN 1-58423-125-4

Designed by Price Watkins
Co-ordinating Research by Jennifer Hudson
Printed in Hong Kong

Frontispiece: Central courtyard of M & C Saatchi in London,
designed by Harper Mackay; see pages 202-7

Acknowledgements/Photograph credits:

The authors would like to thank all the designers and architects involved
and the photographers whose work is reproduced. The following
photographic credits are given, with page numbers in parentheses.

Aker/Zvonkovic Photography (218–19); Arcaid/Nicholas Kane (20–22);
Architekturphoto/Ralph Richters (145 top, 146, 147); Farshid Assassi (15,
18); Paul Bardagjy Photography (47–51); Richard Barnes (143, 208–11);
Hedrich Blessing (128–33); Hedrich Blessing/Chris Barrett (185–9);
Hedrich Blessing/Steve Hall (70–76); Hedrich Blessing/Marco Lorenzetti
(217); Reiner Blunck (38–41); Tom Bonner (16–17, 19); Santi Caleca
(154–5); Louis Casals (56–9); Jeremy Cockayne (52–5); Comstock (182–3);
Richard Davies (45 right); Graeme Duddiridge (34–7); Gerda Eichholzen
(226–7); Mary Evans Picture Library (68–9, 126–7); FLPA/By Silvestris
(12–13); Al Forbes (190–93); Jon Gollings (96–9); Roland Halbe (170–73);
Sam Hecht (200–01); Timothy Hursley (216, 220); Kary Ka-Che Kwok
(42–3, 44 centre, 45 left); Christian Kandzia (163–7); Karant &
Associates/Barbara Karant (30–33); Ian Lambot (144–5, 149); Mitsuo
Matsuoka (169); Voitto Niemela (80–81); Michael O'Callahan Photography
(138–41); Jonathan Pile (212–15); Paul Rattingan (101– 4); Sharon
Risedorph (194–9); Cees Roelofs © Interpolis (24–9); Durston Saylor
(115–19); Shinkenchiku-sha (89, 90); Jussi Tiainen (76–9, 150–53); Jan
Verlinden (110–13); View/Peter Cook (106–9, 120–23, 134–7, 156–61,
175–9); View/Nick Huften (2–3, 202–7); View/Dennis Gilbert (44 left,
60–65, 222–5); Paul Warchol (7, 82–7).

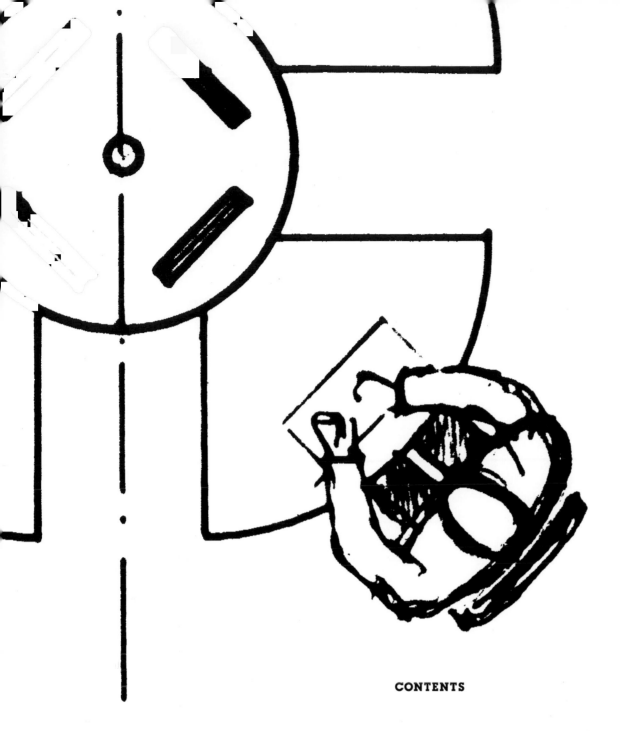

CONTENTS

introduction JEREMY MYERSON AND PHILIP ROSS

CREATIVE OFFICES were once the exclusive province of designers, architects or film-makers; the chic settings for record producers, photographers or fashion people. They belonged to organizations working in the creative industries and were imaginative, alternative and atypical in their style and layout. The vast majority of workplaces meanwhile adhered to a machine-like, hierarchical model of modern office design in which any creative or individual elements were sacrificed to the perceived needs of management efficiency.

Today, growing management interest in new, more informal ways of working has been allied to the rapid emergence of new workplace technologies, especially cordless ones, and innovative approaches to space and architecture. The result is that creative offices are now evident in many different types of business and industry.

The Creative Office charts this dramatic shift. In each of the book's 42 case studies selected from around the world, we have sought to show a named organization occupying and working in a particular location – there are no studies of speculative office buildings or interiors. Of the 40 organizations we have analysed at work in their creative offices, just 40 per cent can be identified as belonging to the creative industries. These firms include TV and film production companies, design and engineering consultants, record labels and specialists in advertising, public relations and fashion.

Sixty per cent of companies featured in this book are corporate or public service organizations traditionally associated with formal and monolithic office environments. They range from computing, car manufacture and telecommunications to furniture, financial services and fast food. They include an aerospace giant (Boeing) and a life science leader (Monsanto) as well as a British government department (the Ministry of Defence). Significantly, some types of organization have escaped our selection; there are no legal firms featured, for example, suggesting the enduring conservatism of this profession.

However for organizations as diverse as Nokia, McDonald's, British Airways, Commerzbank, Rover Group and IBM, the drive towards 'creative officing' – in its many different incarnations and styles – has become a central management preoccupation of the late 1990s. This is especially so for organizations in North America and Britain which provide more than half of all the featured case studies. Germany and Finland are also prominent in exploring alternative workplace interiors, and we include case studies from Japan, Turkey, Italy, Spain, Belgium, the Czech Republic, The Netherlands and Australia, which demonstrate just how much of a global phenomenon the creative office has become in recent years.

Much has been written about why corporate managers and business gurus in the 1990s have become so disenchanted with traditional approaches to office design. Many theories have been expounded on more flexible ways to work and on new physical environments to accommodate and support such change. But apart from a handful of much-publicized landmark projects – most notably the Sol office in Helsinki, the Scandinavian Air Service building just outside Stockholm and the Chiat/Day and Nickelodeon schemes in New York – practical examples of more creative approaches have been thin on the ground.

This book seeks to redress the balance with a host of new examples, the majority completed within the past three years. The choices made by busy, thriving, competitive organizations in terms of space-planning, design, architecture, technology and work style create a composite picture of what the creative office now looks and feels like as we begin a new millennium of work.

FOUR KEY THEMES

These case studies are grouped under four headings: Team, Exchange, Community and Mobility. The Team section looks at offices which encourage team-building and group working. These are not divide-and-rule environments but ones that promote more cognitive work processes and greater interaction between people. The Exchange section explores office environments that are designed to facilitate the building, sharing and presentation of knowledge. Here the collegiate focus of academic and training environments is adapted to the accommodation needs of 'learning organizations'.

The Community section looks at offices that have been planned to foster a spirit of community and promote greater social cohesion. A key focus here is on creating 'town squares', 'neighbourhoods' and 'city streets' within office interiors. The final section – Mobility – examines non-territorial workplaces which offer unprecedented freedom and choice for employees to work where and how they want. There are a range of work settings – from open spaces to private 'cells' – supported by mobile technologies. Every day is different as entirely new work patterns can be created.

Throughout *The Creative Office*, we see environments that aim to support people in thinking more creatively about work – which promote the right-brain skills of intuition, imagination and synthesis, instead of the left-brain focus on rational order, protocol and precedent, which has tended to dictate the shape and style of inflexible scientifically managed offices in the past.

There is no more constructive way to change people's behaviour than to put them in a different environment

Henry Ford once plaintively enquired, 'Why is it that when I buy a pair of hands, I always get a human being as well?'. His inference was that social dynamics got in the way of getting the business done. Fordism and Taylorism, the twin management 'schools' responsible for planning the first factory-offices in the early years of the twentieth century, elevated management goals over individual psychology, reducing people to units of production. Dehumanized time-and-motion studies set the pace and so a pattern was established which has endured for much of this century, bolstered by the modern design ethic which mirrored scientific management theory in its obsession with functionalism.

IMPETUS FOR CHANGE

Today the mould is being broken by organizations which want to use office design to address precisely those issues of social dynamics and individual psychology that Henry Ford, Frederick Taylor and other industrial pioneers sought to suppress. A number of drivers of change are apparent from researching the case studies in this book.

Fundamental cost and competitive pressures are clearly forcing many large, lumbering companies to start behaving like smaller, more agile ones. That means rethinking work methods and locations to become less conglomerate and more focused.

Creating more innovative office environments can realize many tangible business benefits, not least improved efficiency and lower property costs. Dutch insurance company Interpolis, for example, has reduced its property overhead by 20 per cent and relocation by British Airways is forecast to save the airline £15 million a year.

But perhaps the bigger prizes from a more creative approach are those which spring from bringing people together, breaking down barriers between different job functions and departments, improving communication and generating cross-fertilization of ideas. These key objectives are especially pertinent for those firms needing to research, develop and deliver new products. 'Time to market' is a live innovation issue for manufacturers like 3Com and Rover and for consulting firms like IDEO; they all need to shorten the chain of command and speed up decision making.

The need to recruit and retain talented staff in industries where top personnel are at a premium is also a factor driving workplace change. Outperforming the competition is essential and a number of firms are using creative environments to build competitive advantage by attracting the best 'knowledge workers' and giving them the right setting in which to perform.

Companies once determined to keep a lid firmly on change. Now there is a general acceptance – even among established industry leaders – that continuous change is the only constant. Creative offices are widely seen as better able to flexibly absorb the impact of change than monolithic, controlling ones. At Monsanto, for example, there is a recognition that staff must learn to confront change and adapt to survive – with office spaces described as 'meadows', 'porches' and 'parlours' providing familiar reference points to explain a new and unfamiliar work environment (see page 184).

Whereas most traditional offices hinder growth and change, the creative office acts as a catalyst for continuous improvement through learning from experience. For example, a leadership centre built just outside St Louis, Missouri to train Boeing's business leaders of tomorrow will reinforce the company's image as a learning organization (see page 70).

Cultural change can be an immediate beneficiary of physical workplace transformation. There is no more constructive way to change people's behaviour than to put them into a different environment. Removing hierarchy or flattening the pyramid has been a key motivator behind the new workspaces for companies such as Owens Corning, WMA Engineers and the Ministry of Defence's Procurement Executive. British Airways, in seeking to build a stronger customer service focus, used the move to its new Waterside building to rid itself of the remaining vestiges of old Royal Air Force culture where holiday was still called 'leave', the staff ate in the 'mess' and employees still went 'on duty'.

COLLABORATIVE WORKING

Collaboration and team-working also dominate the motives of companies investing in more creative offices. The move towards people working together in multi-disciplinary teams for significant periods of time has led many organizations to create new and dedicated spaces for this to happen effectively. Coley Porter Bell's Visual Planning Room (see page 66) provides a focused environment for teams to work together, as do the Design Council's new offices, where a cross-discipline collaborative approach was central to Ben Kelly's design solution (see page 60). The flux that is common to team-working has been embraced as a challenge as opposed to a problem.

Organizations such as US cable TV company Discovery in Miami (see page 46) have used the environment to deliver constant regrouping as a means of projecting a dynamic culture. Where a business is growing quickly, such as Spanish publishing company Ediciones 62

> Making offices more creative means
> abandoning the old rules about space analysis
> in favour of more generous allocations

(see page 56), increases in headcount can be readily incorporated into an environment built to absorb change.

The need to give people places in which they can feel creative has also been a key motivator. It explains the 'sun spots' at German insurance company LVA, the 'olive grove' at British Airways, the hanging gardens within Commerzbank's tower in Frankfurt or the coloured Edward de Bono brainstorm rooms at Arthur Andersen in London. All provide places to stimulate staff into being creative during their working day.

RANGE OF PROJECTS

The types of projects chronicled in *The Creative Office* are as varied as the organizations themselves and their motives for change. Schemes range from architect-designed 'signature' headquarters (Helin & Siitonen for Nokia, Niels Torp for British Airways, Cesar Pelli for Owens Corning) to refurbishments of historic buildings. In London, for example, an old timber-arched drill hall has become a superb space for record company Independiente (see page 100); in Belgium, a vintage brewery site has been remodelled as an office for engineering firm Seghers (see page 110); in San Francisco, product designers IDEO have occupied a disused waterfront warehouse (see page 194).

Many projects involved relocation due to companies simply outgrowing their space or wanting to streamline several locations into one. Others, such as the refurbishment of Island Records in a Grade II-listed building in St Peter's Square, London, required the designers to renew worn-out services in the existing building (see page 42).

Providing the right service provision proved to be a difficult challenge for many projects, especially those transforming an existing building into something entirely different; Boeing's leadership centre, for example, is a 1952 Carriage House while the new headquarters of Canadian telecommunications company Nortel is a 1963 digital switching factory (see page 128).

NEW WAYS TO PLAN SPACE

Making offices more creative means abandoning the old rules about space analysis and allocation. New approaches to space planning have broken away from the efficiency of the rectangular grid in favour of more innovative and unusual solutions that create unexpected environments within buildings. Where corridors or circulation routes were once straight and narrow, minimized for the sake of efficiency, they are now regarded as valuable spaces and given prominence in workplaces designed to encourage movement and collaboration.

Primary circulation in creative offices is unusually generous, often including spaces for people to meet informally and dwell. These impromptu liaisons will often occur in areas designed for just such an event – at the intersection of converging circulation routes or in a central focal point or atrium space complete with public amenities and, in some cases, works of art.

Planning for interaction is a key trend in the creative office. All the old measures of space planning efficiency – 'density of occupation' or 'net usable space', for instance – are cast aside. Instead there is a transfer of investment and influence from workspace to public space. Areas are generously given to common activities or shared facilities and these central spaces that are publicly owned have been given names to reflect their status. The 'market square', the 'piazza' and the 'street' with its connecting lanes, for example, all describe a new planning paradigm that has redefined space within the workplace and which is often based on the complexity and diversity of the city plan.

RANDOM ENCOUNTERS

It is well known that people working in traditional office buildings rarely interact with each other unless they sit together. In fact, research by telecommunications giant British Telecom found that two people working on different floors in the same building had only a one per cent chance of meeting during any one working day. But as companies move towards a workforce comprised of knowledge workers whose productivity is increased by random encounters that stimulate new ideas and thinking, there is a need to replan the workplace so that these informal and spontaneous meetings can take place relatively easily.

Creative offices provide places for such chance meetings. At British Airways, Rover Group and 3Com, for example, staff can talk and 'trade' in the 'street' without the need to book formal meeting rooms. At the Yapi Kredi bank operations centre in Turkey, a series of streets are based on the medieval traditions of the *Han* and spanned by a fabric roof in keeping with the culture and the climate of the region (see page 174).

Streets imply movement and the concept that people will physically circulate more around their workplace during the day rather than be based in the same place is a recurring trend. The benefits derived from unexpected interaction now override the principles of time-and-motion efficiency that have set people in fixed positions, performing repetitive tasks based in a single location, for much of this century.

The distinction between technology and
physical environment will blur, accelerating
the trend towards flexible working

THRUST FOR VERTICALITY

As well as this changing allocation of space on horizontal floors or planes, the realization that people very rarely move between floors has given way to solutions to bring them together. 'Verticality' is used to describe this trend, demonstrated by the spectacular staircases that punch through floorslabs in buildings to connect floors in such schemes as Bürohaus for a German software company (see page 170) or the Lowe and Partners/SMS advertising office in New York (see page 114). People are given the ability to roam between floors and shared spaces with ease and purpose.

It is interesting that a move towards what appears to be chaotic, irregular space planning still has an order based on modularity. The asymmetry evident in Eva Jiricna's scheme for Andersen Consulting in Prague (see page 106) or Valerio Dewalt Train's for WMA Consulting Engineers in Chicago (see page 30) is actually based on a modular grid that has been used within the organic envelope.

The use of a triangular grid, meanwhile, occurs at Commerzbank in Germany, Nokia in Finland and Pomegranit in California, providing a flexible and effective way of planning the space. At IDEO in San Francisco, at McDonald's in Milan, and in a concept community proposed by designers Morphosis (see page 180), central spines have been used to divide space through an organic structure and introduce natural breaks between the workplace zones.

ANNEXING EXTERNAL SPACE

As well as innovative internal planning, external space is key in the creative office. The use of gardens at British Airways and Commerzbank, central squares at 3Com or water at the Ministry of Defence and Office Daiwa in Japan allows the office to continue beyond the boundaries of the traditional building footprint. This external space has even been 'adopted' by creative companies whose architects have cleverly commandeered external environments to become a part of the workplace.

At M&C Saatchi, the square outside the building has been 'annexed' so that it is perceived to be a part of the arrival. But perhaps the most evident blurring of boundaries is at the Innsbruck Alpine School where a glazed 'container office' has been built in woodland (see page 226). Here the user can drift effortlessly between the internal environment and the external landscape, which in effect becomes a part of the workspace itself.

Unorthodox space planning which allows for more flexible and collaborative working could not be achieved, however, without the powerful enabler of new technology. From cordless communications to the advanced networks and intranets that allow people to connect, technology has changed the way people work in creative offices.

The use of mobile or laptop computers is now widespread and these portable devices allow people to effectively work anywhere within the building or from remote locations. Connecting to the corporate network is a key issue and most companies have provided data ports throughout the work environment, accessible from the desk or table top. However, British Airways has taken connectivity one stage further and introduced a cordless Local Area Network (LAN) that allows laptop computer users to connect through radio waves from anywhere along the central street or even the landscaped gardens around the workplace.

EXPLOITING NEW TECHNOLOGY

The introduction of cordless office telephones has made a dramatic impact. Yesterday's office tied down telephone extensions to desks, linking places together and not people. In the creative office, cordless telephony means that telephones are carried and people can choose to receive or make a call from anywhere in the building. Interpolis gives all 1,500 staff a pocket office telephone, while DEGW and Owens Corning have introduced the system for mobile executives and support staff.

The move towards giving people more control over their local environment has been enabled by new technology that controls a building management system (BMS). At Commerzbank, the naturally ventilated building allows people to open windows for fresh air, but this is complemented by a sophisticated BMS that will automatically shut all windows and switch over to air-conditioning if the outside temperature changes. At Monsanto, staff have portable infra-red controllers that allow them to alter the lighting or heating in the local environment. At Lowe and Partners/SMS, low-energy light fixtures have sensors that respond to the heat and movement of users.

With the relentless penetration of technology into all aspects of the workplace, the creative office has interestingly countered this invasion by also providing places of peace, or 'Zen'. In these islands of 'non-technology' people can concentrate, think, read or write uninterrupted by the mobile telephone, flashing screen or whirring fax.

Since the early 1980s, technology has emerged from the seclusion of the air-conditioned basement computer room guarded by men in white coats to dominate the desktop. It is now set to move to the pocket, where personal communicators will begin to allow people to connect from anywhere, not just for telephone conversations but to receive voice mail, faxes and e-mail as well as access information.

> Creative offices reflect the way organizations
> want to work in the future and redefine everything
> we ever understood about office design

This portability will combine with a corporate infrastructure that will see machines such as laptop computers link to fixed technologies that are embedded within buildings. The Concept Dome Pod, developed for Booz Allen & Hamilton (see page 228), illustrates this migration to a point where the distinction between technology and the physical environment will blur, accelerating the trend towards flexible working and providing the tools for the creative office to become the norm.

LIGHTNESS AND IMMATERIALITY

As if in anticipation of an era of more ubiquitous technology in the workplace, the creative office exhibits particular visual and tactile characteristics. On the evidence of the projects in this book, there is a fascination among workplace architects and designers with transparency and translucency, lightness and immateriality. The message here perhaps is that the physical environment is shedding weight in order to accommodate prodigious amounts of digital technology.

This theme manifests itself in a number of different ways – from the glass office drum with suspended glass table that forms the centrepiece of a scheme for the Simon Jersey uniform maker in Lancashire (see page 52) to the 'floating' *shoji*-style partitions made of rice paper sandwiched between glass at the IBM showroom in Melbourne (see page 96). At Fuel Design in California, technology cabling is open to view in transparent conduits, at M&C Saatchi in London, the partners work at clear glass workbenches; and at Prospect Pictures, also in London, a soft 'light cloister' shields management offices (see page 20).

Coupled with exposed services and ceilings, and expanses of translucent and transparent screening that allow views through and beyond specific work areas, the intervention of autonomous interior elements are a feature of the creative office. Mezzanine levels create their own spatial dynamic at the Independiente record company and at Boeing's leadership centre; a large frosted glass cone is suspended within the interior volume of the Hiratsuka bank in Japan.

If lightness and transparency suggest a monochrome or blanched working world, creative offices are also increasingly big on bright colours – from the red glass bricks and orange walls at the Design Council and the vibrant hues of the custom joinery elements at Island Records to the coloured glass sliding screens in the BGW trade insurance building in Dresden. Once, grey was the model corporate colour. Now primaries are seen as professional too. Personal stimulation is clearly the issue here.

MATERIALS AND METAPHORS

In keeping with a move towards stronger colours, choice of interior materials too suggests the search for more emotional impact. Many schemes elevate natural timbers and fabrics as the workplace materials of choice. The Pomegranit post-production company in San Francisco has redwood ceilings 6 metres (20 feet) high. Redwoods, notably cherry and red oak, feature in the two giant atria which bind together Nokia's headquarters in Espoo – marking a departure from the white modernist halls which characterize most contemporary Finnish architecture. At the Discovery Channel in Miami, recycled timbers and other green and biodegradable materials humanize a highly technical office. Giant trees, shrubs and bushes can be found inside many creative offices, providing not just pleasant decoration but climatic and environmental control too.

While many of the world's largest office furniture manufacturers have products specified for creative offices, the case studies also reveal the limitations of conventional desking to respond to the more fluid contours of new work settings. Custom furniture was designed for a number of projects, including the engineer workstations at Rover in the UK and Seghers in Belgium, flexible furniture at IDEO in Tokyo and a special system of butting tables and desks at Lowe and Partners/SMS in New York.

Perhaps it is not surprising that so many creative office designers should want to craft and shape every element of the workspace rather than simply specify products from a catalogue. The idea of narrative and storytelling has reasserted itself. Scenario and metaphor are a growing feature of the creative office – from the cafés in the Interpolis building which are themed on different world cities to the ornamental gardens at British Airways which are themed on different parts of the world.

The pop art decoration of the McDonald's offices in Milan by Atelier Mendini (see page 154) makes a statement about disposable mass culture, while the distinctive interiors of the high-rise f/X Networks office in Los Angeles provide an ironic commentary on the external views over movie lots, distant hills and the Pacific Ocean.

On the evidence of *The Creative Office*, workplaces are clearly entering a new phase in which personal dreams and visions are no longer systematically crushed by scientific management. The ideas of individuals and of teams are being allowed to flourish in environments which reflect the way organizations want to work in the future and redefine everything we ever understood about using space, form, colour, materials and technology in the modern office interior.

team

OFFICES were once designed to keep people apart. Space planning was based on the ruthless divisions of hierarchy and status. The earliest twentieth-century offices even banned conversation between colleagues. But in the creative office, the important role of the team is at last being recognized. No longer do team solutions rely on occasional use of anonymous meeting rooms or private offices. Dedicated places and spaces that support the cognitive needs of group working over a continuous period are now an integral part of office schemes. Multi-disciplinary teams are being given their own homes which encourage collaboration and interaction, and stimulate creativity and ideas. The following selection of office interiors promote the concept of team.

fuel SHUBIN+DONALDSON ARCHITECTS

FUEL is a young Californian design team with attitude – a specialist in computer animation and digital design which aims to be raw, spontaneous and flexible in its work for such clients as MTV and Pepsi. When it needed space for rapid expansion and moved to a new loft space in a Santa Monica warehouse, it wanted maximum creativity and impact at minimum cost – a technical stronghold for its facilities and a comfortable, style-conscious environment to attract and retain staff in an industry where competition is fierce and the most talented personnel are at a premium.

Architects Shubin+Donaldson have created an engaging scheme which is based on the idea of an 'interior village' of buildings within an autonomous structure. This community has editing bays, animation and production zones, two conference rooms plus a series of small private executive offices and even a miniature 'Zen garden'. But its main focal point is an open-plan activity area complete with indoor basketball hoop and billiard table alongside a kitchen and lounge area where the team can congregate and relax. The play area converts into a studio space for film production.

The entire project was completed to a tight deadline – in just five months from concept to moving in – and cost an economical $322 per square metre ($30 per square foot). Interestingly, the architects used video animation and computer modelling presentation techniques as part of the design process – an approach unusually well suited to this particular client. Perhaps the most distinctive feature of this workplace is its degree of openness expressed in translucent screens, upon which Fuel can project images of its TV commercials and promotional identity work, and transparent conduits that carry technology cabling. The industrial look of the original warehouse, with its concrete and terrazzo floors, has meanwhile been left exposed and intact.

This open and articulate approach allows plenty of light to pass through the interior but also sends an immediate message about the company's expertise in computer graphics and commitment to team-working.

location
santa monica, USA

client
fuel design & production

completed
may 1998

total floor space
740 square metres
(8,000 square feet)

staff
18 people

cost
$240,000

1   Building section

2   The domestic-style den at Fuel's Santa Monica office reflects the need to attract and retain talented young computer animation specialists whose expertise is keenly sought by the industry. High timbered ceilings create loft-like space.

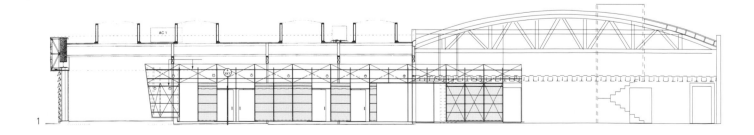

1

2

1   Mezzanine floor plan

2   Main floor plan

3   The main recreational 'play area' at Fuel
    where staff can hang out during
    long working hours. Raw spontaneity is
    a keynote of the scheme.

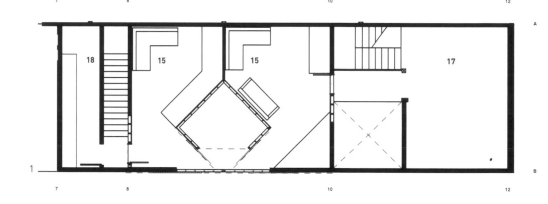

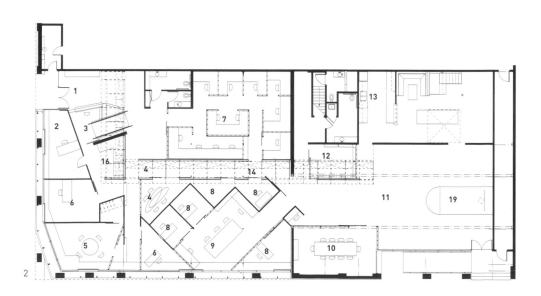

Key
1 Reception 2 Controller
3 Secretarial 4 Small
conference room 5 Director's
office 6 Assistant director's
office 7 Animator/designer bay
8 Producer's office
9 Producer's bay 10 Conference
room 11 Recreation
12 Video vault 13 Kitchen
14 Info bar hall 15 Video edit bay
16 Copy/file 17 Lounge
18 Storage 19 Basketball

2

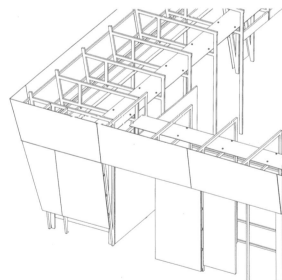

3

1 The use of translucent screens
   enables open vistas through
   the Fuel workplace.

2 The producers' bay: informal
   work areas combine comfort
   with brisk professionalism.

3 Design detail of the Info bar
   hall: the project revels in the
   language of construction.

prospect pictures   BUSCHOW HENLEY

DESIGNERS Buschow Henley have an acknowledged interest and expertise in office design for team-working on account of their much-publicized scheme for London media company Michaelides & Bednash, which was based around a 20 metre (66 foot) long single refectory-style table accommodating every single member of staff. This project for another burgeoning firm in the heart of the UK creative industry also solves the problems of team space – but in a strikingly different way.

The main issue in creating a new office, editing facilities and TV studio for Prospect Pictures was in resolving high-density occupation of a six-storey 1950s building. The solution has been to divide the building into three distinct 'worlds': TV studio and edit suites in the basement; management and administration on the ground and first floors; and open rooms for the itinerant freelance production teams who develop programmes on the upper floors.

To achieve the density levels required, it was important to position as carefully as possible four servicing monoliths, carrying light, power, IT and telephone connections, and to sub-divide the space as little as possible. Within the building, the designers have created a series of simple white volumes enlivened by light-emitting and material installations. Service points provide local markers to which teams gravitate.

On the ground floor, a glazed shopfront and stone floor link the main street outside to a rear courtyard long since enclosed to provide additional space and transformed into a pair of interlocking meeting rooms lit by a rooflight. On this level, a soft, wood-framed structure clad in GRP acts as a 'light cloister', forming a series of quiet retreat spaces. A 'colour wall' of red, green and blue light (the colours that constitute a TV picture) further shields the management offices from the street. On the first floor, offices double as meeting rooms.

Below, studio and edit suites are directly linked to the management activity. Above, the freelance production team floors, each about 80 square metres (860 square feet) in size, have been designed to accommodate up to sixteen people in comfort – typically, four teams of four, two teams of eight, or one of sixteen, each team grouped around a service monolith. This is a scheme in which the requirement for high levels of technical and team integration has been met with elegance and grace.

location
london, UK

client
prospect pictures

completed
august 1996

total floor space
750 square metres
(8,070 square feet)

staff
variable (45 maximum)

cost
undisclosed

1

1   Management offices at Prospect
    Pictures are shielded from the
    street by this soft, wood-framed
    'colour wall'.

2   A view into the kitchen area
    reveals the interior's bold
    colours and finishes, which lend
    the scheme refinement.

2

1 Ground floor management office: creating a sense of calm despite high-density use, with special attention to storage.

2 Typical upper floor plan

3 Ground floor plan

4 Axonometric: basement edit suites and upper floor production team spaces sandwich ground and first floor management areas.

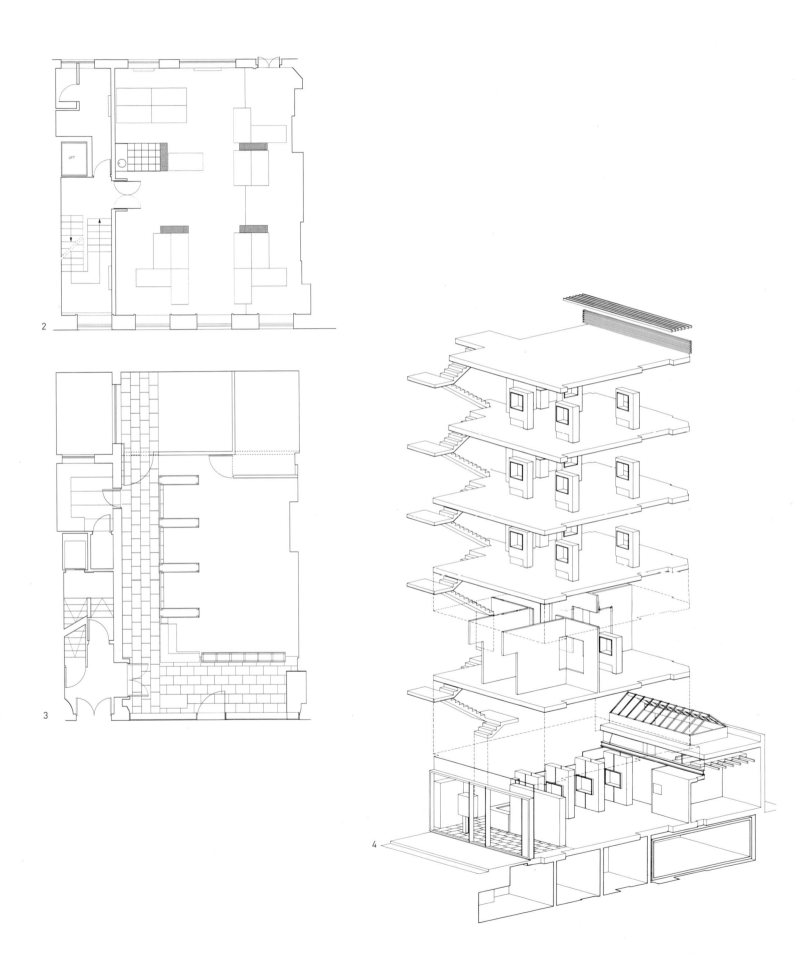

1

2

3

4

interpolis   ABE BONNEMA

FOR an insurance company to embrace new ways of working is fairly common, but for one to build new landmark headquarters based on workplace change and the latest technology is certainly unusual. For Dutch insurance company Interpolis, however, the investment in providing a flexible, high-tech, team-based environment has resulted in a 30 per cent saving in property costs.

Architect Abe Bonnema proposed a high-rise building close to Tilburg's business district with a low-rise annexe incorporating an extensive entrance hall. The tower was designed with small floor plates just 12 metres (40 feet) across, so that the structure could be supported by its walls and not by beams or columns. This created 20 team-based floors that can be rearranged at will using moveable partitions.

Additional flexibility is due to innovative technology. A computer-based intranet system allows users to check who is in the building or video-conference with reception to check if their visitor has arrived. A cabling system links laptop computers to a network, and a cordless telephone system allows people to be contacted wherever they are in the facility while freeing up the space from unsightly wires.

The interior of each team floor provides Interpolis staff with a choice of work settings. As they enter the floor, employees check their pigeonholes, pick up their cordless telephones and collect their 'flexi-cases' containing their personal effects. They then either select a private 'cockpit' for concentrated work or one of a number of open areas to work on the task at hand.

Each team space has its own identity, dramatically visualized by a café at the entrance to each floor designed as a different world city – from Rio to Barcelona. The environment is open and light, with use of glazed partitions and natural wood specified by interior designers Kho Liang Ie Associates to create a restful and informal atmosphere.

People are also encouraged to work in common areas of the building in line with the Interpolis philosophy that 'your place of work is wherever you happen to be'. This area includes the spectacular entrance hall, with its perforated metal units and information pillars, the restaurant and landscaped garden featuring unusual sculptures. Dutch insurance companies have a pedigree in office design dating back to Herman Hertzberger's 1973 Centraal Beheer scheme at Apeldoorn. But this Interpolis project writes an entirely new chapter on ways to work.

location
tilburg, the netherlands

client
interpolis

architect
abe bonnema, bureau for architecture and environmental planning BV

workplace consultants
veldhoen facility consultants

interior designers
kho liang ie associates

completed
november 1997

total floor space
11,610 square metres
(125,000 square feet)

staff
1,500 people

cost
£56 million

1

2

1　An undulating metal structure provides a
　　dramatic arrival into the main entrance hall
　　where public and meeting areas give way
　　to security access to the office floors above.

2　The Interpolis building's high-rise office block
　　and its adjacent service tower stand above
　　the main entrance and amenities annexe.
　　The garden's slate collage is in the foreground.

1   Typical office block floor plan. The service tower
    is reached via a spectacular glass bridge. The
    office floor shows a combination of private
    cockpits and open-plan spaces together with
    centralized storage and a corner café.

2   A corner café at the entrance to the team office
    floor provides an informal place to meet, themed
    to reflect a world city – in this case New York.

3   Informal meeting area within the ground floor
    reception space. A semicircular perforated metal
    screen provides a degree of privacy while
    ensuring that the space remains open and public.

Overleaf
    View of a team work area in the office block
    showing open-plan workstations made by Samas
    together with an informal meeting area on
    a red sofa. The idiosyncratic light sculpture and
    suspended lighting disc soften the environment.

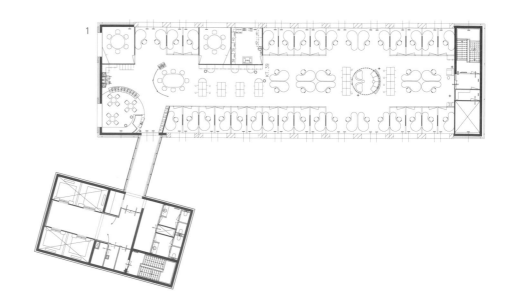

WMA VALERIO DEWALT TRAIN ASSOCIATES

FROM the moment of entry into the Chicago office of engineering firm WMA through an iconic stainless steel rotunda inexpensively fabricated in sheet metal, this is a workplace that is determined to minimize hierarchy and status and promote interaction between the company's professional staff. Designers Valerio Dewalt Train, well known for a series of imaginative US Robotics offices in the Illinois area, have turned a two-storey loft renovation into an innovative setting for group work. The entire scheme builds up from the basic component of the individual engineer's workstation. This has been custom designed to accommodate the computers, drawings and reference materials needed on a continual basis. The desk is U-shaped, measuring 2.4 by 3 metres (8 by 10 feet) and made in modest materials – raw medium-density-fibreboard finished in polyurethane for the tops, birch plywood units dyed and finished with lacquer for support panels and shelving.

There are 55 of these workstations fitted into the building's small structural bays, with low dividing walls to facilitate project team communication. They fill an open room punctuated by service towers housing copiers, printers and libraries and rising to a height of 6.7 metres (22 feet). Each workstation is a module which repeats to form a grid of blocks and streets. Running alongside this area is a layer of partners' offices and on the opposite side a small tier of project managers' offices.

If all this sounds like the kind of rational office planning to be expected in a scheme for engineers, then the diagonally juxtaposed layout of the lighting is the element that really pushes this project out of the ordinary. A medley of specially adapted indirect fittings and custom-fabricated wall-mounted light boxes shines light off suspended stainless steel partitions and exposed services to animate the loft-height space, so creating a genuinely communal corporate culture. As designer Joe Valerio admits: 'The design goes nutty in the third dimension'.

WMA's new workplace was designed to accommodate the rapid expansion that had seen the company increase its fee income by a quarter for each of the past four years. On an upper floor a further 465 square metres (5,000 square feet) has been partially fitted out so that it too can be swiftly given the same idiosyncratic high-finish, low-budget treatment as WMA recruits more staff to its showcase office.

location
chicago, USA

client
WMA consulting engineers

completed
december 1996

total floor space
2,135 square metres
(23,000 square feet)

staff
60 people

cost
$750,000

1

1 Work room illuminated by a diagonally juxtaposed medley of custom light fittings.

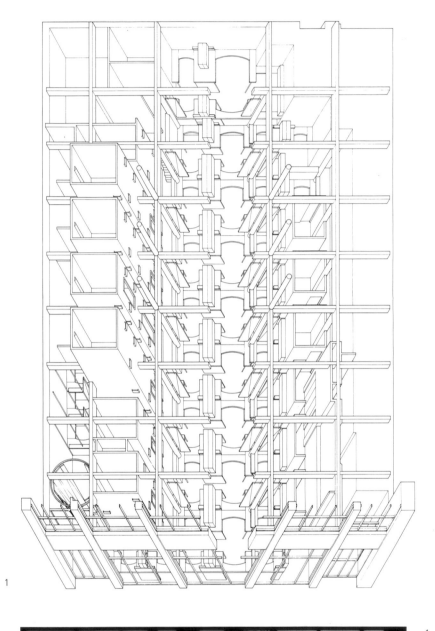

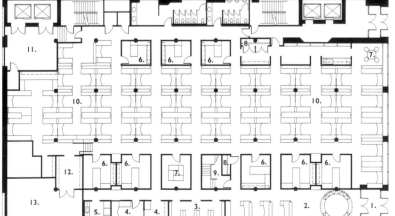

1 Axonometric shows the
  engineering of the building
  stripped bare.

2 Main floor plan

3 Views into and through the
  stainless steel entrance rotunda,
  which was specially fabricated
  for the project by a ductwork
  manufacturer.

3

1 Entry
2 Reception
3 Library
4 Computer room
5 Kitchen
6 Office
7 Conference
8 Closet
9 Stair
10 Workroom
11 Deliveries
12 Storage
13 Mechanical

mission   MISHA STEFAN

TUCKED into London's Westbourne Grove district is a fashionable design gallery called Mission – its title an amalgam of the names of its founders, architect Misha Stefan and his partner Yvonne Courtney. And tucked into the back of the Mission gallery is a jewel of a small team office designed by Stefan for Courtney Communications, Yvonne Courtney's PR company.

This low-budget project creates a soft and womb-like working environment using curved walls and doors, round windows and sculptured elements, gently lit and coloured in whites and pastel greens. The effect is of an enclosed subterranean world complete with recessed wall shelving to provide streamlined storage and ceiling sky-lights which introduce natural light to the below-deck ambience.

Stefan's scheme has three main elements: a fluid-form workspace with wall-facing workstations and Eames chairs for 'hot desking'; a meeting room with a table that slides into the floor to become a shelf; and three separate offices. Its quality resides in its pleasing spatial relations, volumes and details – a lighting switch is part of the handrail at the entrance, for example. A palette of plaster, wood, glass, paint and plywood has been worked to good effect, achieving a sophistication of style on a very low budget.

Beyond the Courtney Communications office, the compact Mission gallery itself extends the soft and organic mood in a delightful, gently unfolding way. But it is the creative team space at the hub of the gallery – a behind-the-scenes operation which has been celebrated in design rather than sacrificed to save costs – that really signals Mission's commitment to quality.

location
london, UK

client
courtney communications

completed
september 1997

total floor space
110 square metres
(1,200 square feet)

staff
6 people

cost
undisclosed

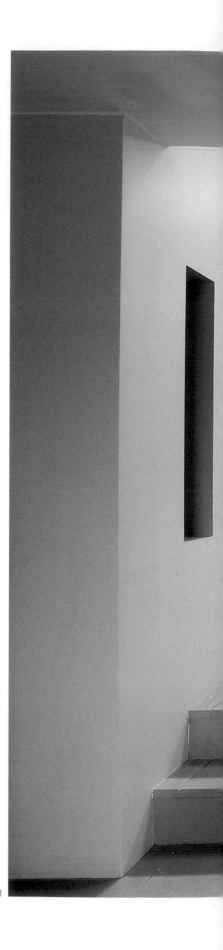

1   A hot-desking area in the organically formed Mission office. Space is precious and used economically to effect. Environmental controls are built into the flowing curve of the plaster balustrade.

1 Floor plan

2 Section

3 Small sunken meeting area
  serviced by a small kitchen.
  Soft colours and smooth
  finishes suggest an enclosed
  subterranean world.

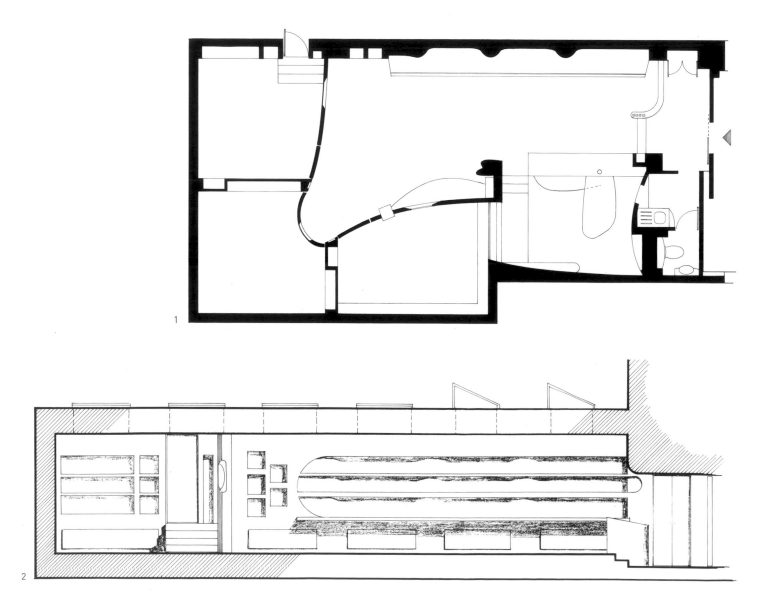

1

2   3

B G W **LOG ID**

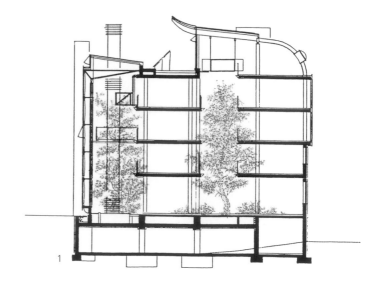

FOUNDED in 1929, the BGW (Berufsgenossenschaft für Gesundheitsdienst und Wohlfahrtspflege) is a German trade accident insurance company. It is responsible for about 420,000 businesses with more than five million insured employees. As a company that aims to prevent accidents at work and the growth of occupational diseases, it is understandably eager to promote best practice in office design.

This Dresden office block, designed by LOG ID, is one of the BGW's 12 regional centres across Germany. Much of its innovation and creativity is expressed in the technical invention of its green architecture: its curved roof opens to the south to establish a relationship with the sun; ceiling-hung translucent panels in the four-storey glass-box structure combat glare and heat build-up as part of a seasonally adjustable natural solar ventilation system; rainwater irrigates subtropical plants which provide natural shading; and photo-voltaic panels on the roof reduce the building's reliance on the main energy supply.

There is also much to admire in the way the interior is fitted to the work style and ethos of the organization. The architects were determined to promote staff interaction by avoiding massive dividing walls and anonymous corridors. Open-plan workspace is divided by tall cabinet elements and by individually movable sliding screens of coloured glass in front of offices on the glass-walled south side of the building, which make it possible to adjust the lighting and work undisturbed. This flexible and open approach makes the space multi-purpose in that individual offices can be quickly reconfigured into team spaces, with media access, light and power supply.

The inevitable acoustic problems arising from this concept have been countered by acoustic plastering of ceilings, by carpeting all offices and by an abundance of indoor plants, which reduce noise levels as well as creating a sense of well-being. Natural building materials (for example, maple parquet floors) have been specified throughout the project, and smart kitchenettes have been integrated into the main business areas.

Corkscrew-shaped staircases vertically thread through the different levels of the Dresden BGW building, while views from the main platforms and landings link the interior to the open, green parkland near the centre of the old city which provides an apt setting for this energy-efficient and user-friendly office.

location
dresden, germany

client
BGW – employers' health and welfare association

completed
november 1996

total floor space
4,000 square metres
(43,050 square feet)

workplaces
140

cost
DM19 million

1 Section reveals the role of giant tropical plants in this 'green' building's natural system of heating and ventilation.

2 Exterior view

3 Buffer area between the offices on the south side of the building and the façade. Movable coloured glass screens control light and provide privacy. Spiral staircases create vertical circulation between levels.

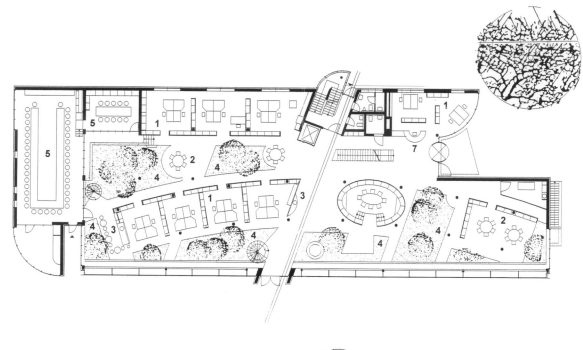

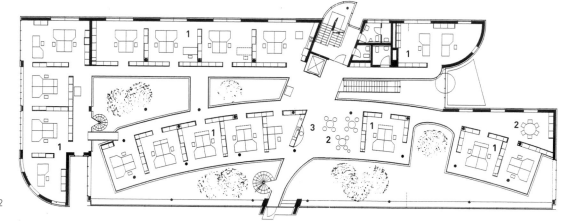

Key
1 Flexible office
  space
2 Meeting
3 Tea point
4 Planting
5 Conference
6 Library
7 Reception

1 Ground floor plan

2 First floor plan

3 View into ground floor
   oval library, just one
   of the scheme's many
   distinctive features.

3

island records   POWELL-TUCK ASSOCIATES

THE culture that sustains a record company tends to be more relaxed and less corporate than for other organizations. But behind the laid-back style, the record company office nevertheless has to function effectively, maintain team spirit and incorporate new technology.

The west London headquarters of Island Records is a good case in point. An 1830s private house originally built as part of the Grade II-listed St Peter's Square development backing on to another nineteenth-century local landmark (the former Chiswick Laundry Building) has been Island's suitably informal home since the early 1970s. But by the early 1990s it had become run down, spatially inefficient, full of redundant services and ill-equipped to deal with new technology.

The task of designers Powell-Tuck Associates was to untangle the services and make the building work more efficiently without destroying the essential culture of the company within the headquarters. The conversion work was carried out over two years in six phases. Through replanning space and circulation, 12 new purpose-designed workstations have been introduced for Island staff and an extra 575 square metres (6,200 square feet) of office space made available to sister companies within the Polygram group. Behind the scenes, essential service renewal has been carried out.

But what really makes this scheme distinctive is the way that no two office spaces are the same within the building. Each affords a degree of privacy while remaining in close physical and visual contact with the whole. Departmental territories have been formed at different levels by purpose-made joinery elements which provide much new storage throughout the building. A range of bright colours enliven the interior, especially in circulation areas and on the new joinery. In this scheme technical requirements have produced a strikingly creative response.

location
london, UK

client
island records

completed
june 1996

total floor space
1,300 square metres
(13,995 square feet)

staff
100 people

cost
£1 million

1

2

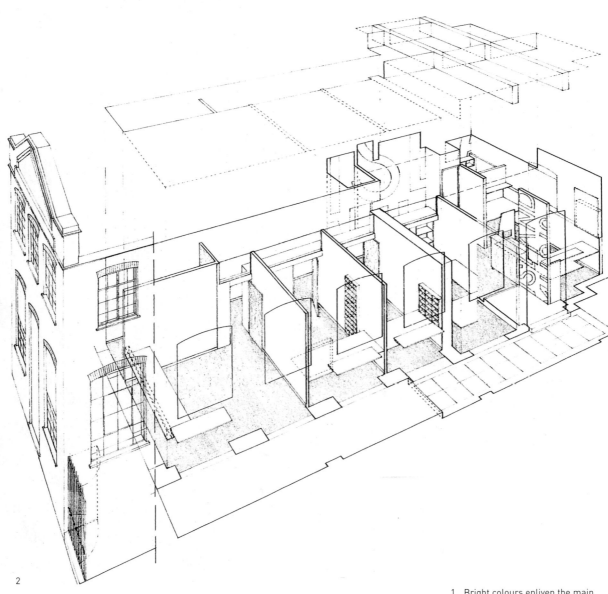

1 Bright colours enliven the main
   corridor at Island Records.

2 Axonometric shows the creation of
   new office space in a Grade II-listed
   house dating from the 1830s.

3

1 A sleek new look in the public areas masks the renewal of essential technical services at Island Records.

2 Custom joinery creates versatile storage in the managing director's office.

3 Main staircase: company culture is reflected in the modernized environment.

discovery channel STUDIOS ARCHITECTURE

JUST across the road from Miami International Airport, a three-storey building has been converted into cable provider Discovery Communications' Latin America Television Centre, in a project that, unusually, combines high technology with recycled timbers. The result is a human and engaging scheme in which technical sophistication goes hand in hand with an informal, task-orientated team approach.

Discovery's emergence as a major broadcasting company necessitated the new state-of-the-art digital TV facility, which now broadcasts seven channels simultaneously in three languages, 24 hours a day to South America and the Iberian peninsula. Not only did the project need to accommodate sensitive audio and video production areas, but team space was required for more than 200 creative and marketing staff who provide the programming for the channels.

A feature of Discovery's work style is constant regrouping and collaborating in work-break areas as part of the dynamic ideas-orientated culture of the company. The designers were initially asked to focus on space for advertising and sales staff but the project subsequently expanded to encompass the entire Miami facility. Virtual reality modelling on computer was a key part of the development process, enabling client and consultancy to explore an accurate depiction of the look and feel of the space.

The key to Studios' scheme is the use of 'green materials' such as natural timbers to soften the hard edges associated with high technology, to create visual landmarks and to guide circulation within the building. A monumental stair tower made of timber trusses protrudes on to the atrium, connecting the three floors of the facility and acting as its hub. At all three levels, a red wall slicing at a diagonal visually links this stair hub to the floor entry point.

Wherever possible, Studios specified eco-friendly materials, salvaging timbers from demolished structures, using biodegradable surfacing and flooring materials such as linoleum, and eliminating the suspended ceiling to reduce the amount of material at ceiling level. The design is not simply a moral essay about sustainability – the paramount image is a celebration of the broadcast function with edit suites and video production areas open to corridors lined with monitors showing current programming. But this is a project which never forgets that teams of people make programmes, not rows of machines.

location
miami, USA

client
discovery channel latin america/iberia

completed
march 1999

total floor space
6,690 square metres
(72,000 square feet)

staff
over 200 people

cost
undisclosed

1 Suspended TV screens and soft seating in a main production thoroughfare. The scheme is environment friendly, making extensive use of recycled timbers and biodegradable flooring.

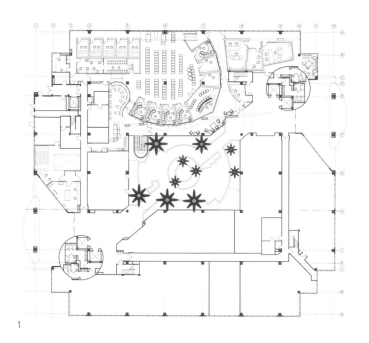

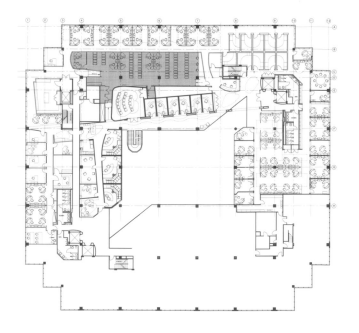

1

2

3

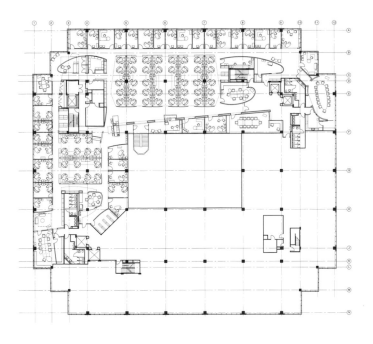

1   Ground floor, second floor
    and third floor plans

2   High technology humanized in a
    public meeting space which looks on
    to the ground floor atrium, with its
    tropical plants.

3   View of storage units in open work
    area: sustainable design was a mission
    of the project.

4   Typical workstation at Discovery
    Channel. Made by Haworth, the Crossings
    system puts accent on flexible working
    and ease of use.

1 The heart of the machine:
   Discovery Channel production
   suite, in use 24 hours a day.

2 View from inside the atrium of
   the main stair tower which
   connects all three floors of the
   facility and acts as its hub.

simon jersey co. STUDIO BAAD

ARCHITECT Philip Bintliff of Studio BAAD regards office buildings as 'permanently in progress' rather than frozen pinnacles of perfection that can never be changed. His practice's work with client Simon Jersey, a successful British manufacturer of work-wear for business and industry, is a case in point. Studio BAAD first completed an office building for Simon Jersey in 1988. The company expanded rapidly and a second building four times its size was completed in 1992.

In the latest phase of work – a response to staffing levels exceeding 300 – Simon Jersey has been revisited yet again. This time around, the architect has designed a drumlike office extension three storeys high in part, a new kitchen extension and an extension to an existing garment storage and distribution area (used for research and development). Also extended has been a design vocabulary that has stayed fresh and animated despite the evident familiarity between architect and workplace client.

Transparency, light and variety are the keynotes. The project features a purpose-designed structural glazing system utilizing clear glass bonded to American ash frames. There is also a spectacular suspended glass table and structural glass floors in the three-storey office 'drum'; these elements serve to bring natural light to the lower ground floor offices built partly backed to earth and below ground. A staircase with glass threads, itself a technical tour de force, links the three floors of the naturally ventilated office drum.

The extended garment store, accommodating the design, quality control and inspection teams, introduces a free-standing translucent glazed wall on its western elevation, shaded by external fabric sails on six steel tripods to reduce the amount of light. This self-supporting element can be relocated to permit further expansion – the architect has learnt through experience that Simon Jersey never stands still for long.

This is a project with a visual richness and eclecticism that comes from the willingness of the designers to create a workplace of transient theatricality that is also intensely practical for an ever-burgeoning business. Team spaces, for example, have giant blow-ups from the Simon Jersey catalogue. Public facilities such as meeting areas and thoroughfares close to WCs have been designed to encourage chance encounters – although now that the company has grown so much, nothing is left to chance and the organization is fully networked with welcome computer screens programmed to feature company news and information each morning.

location
accrington, UK

client
simon jersey co.

completed
july 1998

total floor space
2,900 square metres
(31,215 square feet)

staff
over 300 people

cost
£1.5 million

1

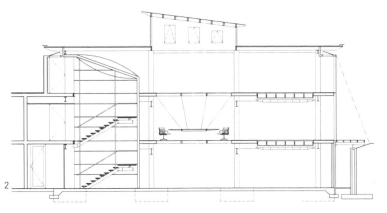

1 An extended garment store becomes a spectacular team setting for design, research and development. Simon Jersey catalogue blow-ups are used on storage units.

2 Section showing the suspended glass table in the three-storey glass office drum.

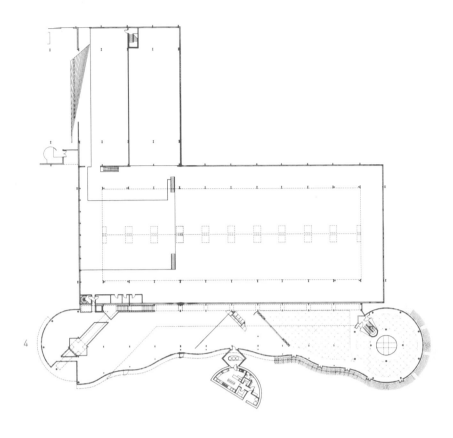

1 Fabric sails on the western
elevation reduce the amount
of light flooding into the
research and development
area. This tripod-supported
element is removable to
allow for future expansion.

2 An eye-shaped hall leads
to WCs. Every corner of the
scheme exudes creative
thinking.

3 The suspended glass table
is a technical tour de force.

4 Plan of the building, with
the extended garment store
shielded by external fabric
sails shown top left.

ediciones 62

LLUIS PAU/MARTORELL-BOHIGAS-MACKAY

TEAMWORK matters more in some industries than in others. In publishing, it is crucial. Spanish publishing company Ediciones 62 has been located in the Raval district of Barcelona since its building was created in 1992 from six adjoining commercial units. When the company expanded, a new interior office scheme was sought, which would be capable of reconciling the long, thin, rectangular plan of the office with the organizational demands of publishing.

Interior designers Lluis Pau/Martorell-Bohigas-Mackay have located the company on two newly designed floors within this elongated architectural container, which has openings all around its perimeter and is accessible via its main longitudinal façade. The 650 square metre (7,000 square foot) ground floor is divided into three main areas to reflect the three key components of the company. In the centre, there is general and editorial management and literary publishing. To the right, there is a bookshop and its sales teams; to the left, administration and computer services. These areas enjoy a degree of autonomy but are also part of the organization as a whole.

A 570 square metre (6,135 square foot) mezzanine floor holds reference and illustration material as well as magazines. This mezzanine is set back three metres (nine feet) from the external longitudinal façade, creating a double-height space to act as the ground-level public thoroughfare. Throughout the scheme, there is an open team environment which incorporates new technology, enabling a company originally founded in 1962 to work in a state-of-the-art setting with networked communications.

The project is robust looking, featuring industrial light reflectors and galvanized steel. There is also a collage of under-valued and environment-friendly materials, including chipboard, melamine and vegetable fibre shavings. This combination of the contemporary with the company's original 1960s furniture gives Ediciones 62 an unusual and effective workplace that is as open as it is long.

location
barcelona, spain

client
ediciones 62

completed
february 1997

total floor space
1,175 square metres
(12,650 square feet)

staff
65 people

cost
£405,100

1 Ground floor bookshop and informal sales area. Classic 1960s furniture, seen as part of the original pioneering spirit of the company, was retained in the new scheme.

1

1 View from the mezzanine
   level down the long, narrow
   interior of the building.

2 Sections and floor plans
   reveal how this publishing
   company has organized its
   activities within one long
   continuous tube. The ground
   floor plan (bottom) divides
   up the space according
   to three discrete functions.

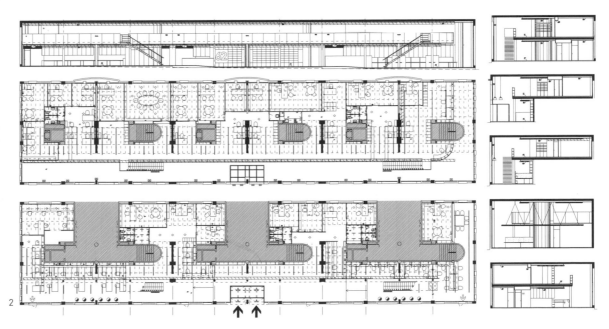

design council   BEN KELLY DESIGN

WHEN the Design Council in Britain was reshaped and relaunched as
a smaller and more proactive campaigning body with a remit to 'inspire
the best use of design in a world context', an inspirational new headquarters was needed to reflect its new role. The state-funded body
which once employed more than 200 people was slimmed down to just
40 core staff, with a mission to collaborate with external partners
across government, business and education.

Its existing headquarters in London's Haymarket House – the
Design Council's home since the 1950s – was deemed no longer suit-
able for its new collaborative, team-based work style and a search was
instigated to find new premises. The solution was found on the third
and fourth floors of a somewhat brutalist 1960s telephone exchange
building in the Covent Garden area of London, which overlooks the
redeveloped Royal Opera House.

Within 1,860 square metres (20,000 square feet) of light industrial
space, interior designer Ben Kelly has created a flexible and often
exciting team environment. The main open-plan work area is to be
found on the third floor, which is punctuated by giant telegraph poles
and makes dramatic use of its 4.2 metre (14 foot) floor-to-ceiling
height. Massive, sliding screens divide the front half of the floor into a
series of multi-functional spaces – café, reception, waiting, exhibition
and seminar areas – or one large space with a servery at one end.

A central staircase punches through the floor slab up to the fourth
floor which is dedicated to more private activities. Facilities include two
glass-fronted meeting rooms, a library and a preparation area for visuals. Throughout the scheme, Ben Kelly's trademark juxtaposition of
unusual materials and striking colours is much in evidence. There is a
semicircular wall of red glass bricks; light fittings which resemble
seagulls, flying saucers and flying carpets; and a curious Norwegian
chalet-style 45 square metre (500 square
foot) wooden entrance on the ground floor.

The impact of select dashes of decorative
colour and wit together with the overriding
principles of light and space – making maximum use of windows on three sides of the
building – is to create a working office which
is stimulating and fun to be in. Its openness
enhances communication – not just for core
staff but for external collaborators who are
such important members of the Design
Council teams.

location
london, UK

client
design council

completed
january 1998

total floor space
1,860 square metres
(20,000 square feet)

staff
40 people

cost
£1.5 million

2

1 The post and service room has been given
   distinction with unusual colours and materials,
   including a red glass brick wall.

2 The main third floor open-plan work area
   illustrates Ben Kelly's transformation of an old
   telephone exchange into a dramatic new
   home for the Design Council. Light fittings are
   mounted on old telegraph poles (left).

1

1 The Design Council café doubles as all-day work and meeting space, and opens on to an exhibition area.

2 Third floor plan: fixed work areas to the left contrast with a series of multi-functional spaces to the right.

3 View of main wooden staircase which punches through the floor slab from third to fourth level. Extensive use is made of timber detailing in this interior.

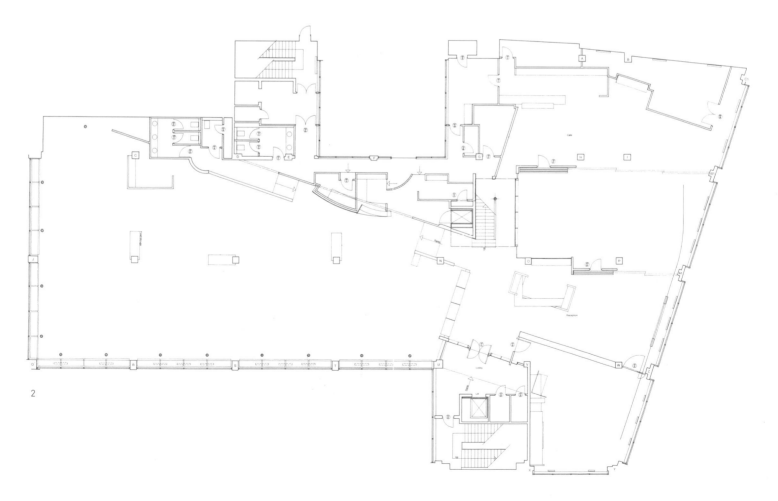

2

3

1 Ground floor wooden
entrance booth to the
Design Council: an
awkward space is turned
to advantage as a
promotional showcase
for the organization's
activities.

2 Fourth floor meeting
room: making teams
work effectively was
a key part of the Design
Council brief.

1

coley porter bell
visual
planning area

APICELLA ASSOCIATES

THIS concept was developed by Apicella Associates for the London offices of brand and packaging design consultancy Coley Porter Bell.

The Visual Planning Area is a team space that has been designed to stimulate creativity during the design development process. It provides clients, consumers and the project team with a dedicated and inspiring space where brainstorming and concept development can take place.

The space itself takes ownership of the ideas and thought process generated by members of the team, who work together or in smaller groups over a number of days. The flexibility of the space allows for this process to unfold and tracks the development of ideas that remain displayed on boards and walls during the visual planning process. It is well known that the presence of familiar objects and imagery stimulates memory; this space builds on this premise to create an effective think-tank in which people can work together.

Shown here is an interior view and section of the Visual Planning Area reflecting patterns of team interaction.

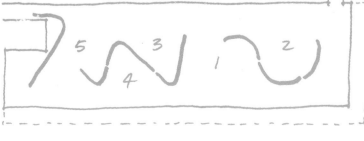

OFFICES were once paper factories dedicated to repetitive processes. Information was hoarded, not shared. Strict division of labour precluded any real interchange of knowledge or ideas. But in the creative office, the linear processing of the traditional company is giving way to a more fluid, progressive approach in which knowledge is power – to be built, bartered, shared and transferred. In this spirit of exchange, office environments are taking on many of the traits of universities: learning is taking place within organizations by virtue of them having the space and facilities to develop. The following selection of office interiors allow the free exchange of ideas.

excha

nge

boeing leadership centre

HELLMUTH, OBATA + KASSABAUM

AEROSPACE giant Boeing, a global leader in its industry, is very committed to being a learning organization. In October 1996 it acquired a 706 hectare (286 acre) country estate on the Missouri River 15 miles north of St Louis to be the site of a flexible and professional learning centre for all of the company's current and future leaders. By the year 2000 this residential training centre will operate complete with extensive workshops, dining and fitness areas, and 120 lodge rooms.

This project represents a first giant step towards the overall goal. Architectural practice HOK was commissioned to restore an existing 1952 Carriage House on the site to act as an interim learning facility. This environment, designed to encourage highly collaborative work, has become 'the hot place to meet' throughout Boeing. Many of its users have commented that it forces them to approach problems from a different angle, 'to think outside the box'.

Within the original limestone-clad structure of the French Revival-style Carriage House, with its views of rivers, farmland, woods and wetlands, HOK has inserted a mezzanine suspended from the building's structural system of glue-laminated beams. This extra 275 square metre (2,970 square foot) space, in addition to the 520 square metre (5,600 square foot) ground floor, means that a wide range of constantly changing learning events and curricular activities can be accommodated in the learning centre.

State-of-the-art communication technology has been embedded into this modified structure to enhance the learning experience. Furniture and equipment were selected for mobility and adaptability to multiple tasks. Most are on castors, permitting greater spontaneity. After a day of meetings users can roll the furniture out of the way to create space for an evening reception. Four leading US furniture manufacturers – Herman Miller, Knoll, Haworth and Steelcase – contributed to the project.

Boeing describes the leadership centre as a 'crossroads, a place where leaders at all levels come at key transition points in their careers to learn, share ideas and exchange best practice'. The approach to design taken by HOK creates a modern and dynamic workplace within the context of an old-fashioned rural setting. This means that Boeing managers have the best of both worlds – an opportunity to get up to speed on the latest management thinking in an environment with the space and stimuli to ensure that the message really sinks in.

1 Exterior view of the 1952 Carriage House transformed into a learning centre for Boeing, the first staging post in plans to create a large state-of-the-art training campus on the site.

2 View from the mezzanine of the multifunctional interior space of the Leadership Centre. Furniture and equipment were specified for their mobility.

location
st louis, missouri, USA

client
the boeing company

completed
february 1997

total floor space
795 square metres
(8,570 square feet)

staff
variable (50 maximum)

cost
undisclosed

1

2

1　Ground floor plan

2　Mezzanine floor plan

3　Staircase to mezzanine level.
　Highly engineered Aeron
　chairs by Herman Miller lend
　a flavour of technology to
　an environment that is
　deliberately low-tech and
　flexible in form and materials.

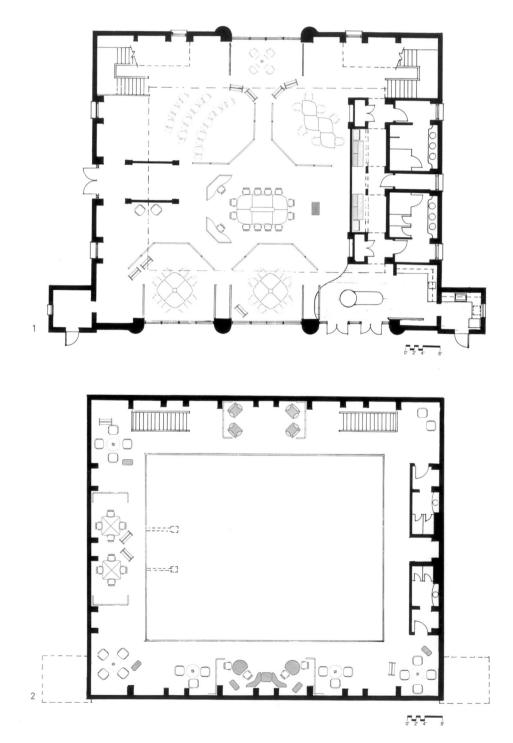

1

2

3

1 Gateway to the great
   outdoors in the Boeing
   Leadership Centre.
   Workspaces look towards
   the external environment
   of woods and wetlands
   for inspiration.

2 A domestic-style
   sit-down area for Boeing's
   future leaders to relax and
   reflect on the learning
   process. Materials are
   light and natural.
   Technology is never overt.

1

n o k i a **HELIN & SIITONEN ARCHITECTS**

PEKKA HELIN and Tuomo Siitonen deserve extra marks for perseverance in the design of Nokia House. It is not simply that their landmark office scheme for the telecommunications company relates well to its spectacular landscape setting on a peninsular near Tapiola. Nor that their interior design uses large quantities of red-hued wood to replace the white central halls typical of modern Finnish architecture with a warmer working environment.

The fact is that the architects have won the project in Espoo not once but twice. Their first competition-winning proposal, in 1983, was postponed on grounds of cost and planning appeals. By the time the need for a new headquarters building for Nokia was reviewed a decade later, the operational structure of the company had changed.

Nokia had become a more focused, knowledge-driven organization in which creative thinking and interaction were essential. A second architectural competition in 1994/5 was again won by Helin & Siitonen, their scheme reflecting the aim for a versatile working environment in which communication is enhanced and knowledge shared.

A spatial plan based on triangles is grouped around two impressive central atria. Each triangular planning unit of 1,000 square metres (10,760 square feet) is repetitive and easily altered, and caters for both individual and group work, with fixed structures and installations kept to a minimum. Throughout the space there are 20 different triangles, containing such elements as cellular offices, meeting rooms, landscaped desking areas and storage areas. One triangle can house between 40 and 80 members of staff, with layout designed to foster chance 'positive encounters' between them.

The two central atria act as vibrant public assembly spaces at ground level, housing a restaurant, meeting place and exhibition areas. Private rooms and meeting rooms for use by outside visitors are sited on this level. But what really distinguishes the scheme is the choice of interior materials. These support the knowledge-exchange workstyle objectives of the project, chiefly through a range of redwoods used with grey-painted steel and glass. On the ground floor, cherry and red oak feature. On floors above ground level, furniture, doors and wall elements are made of common alder and birch. This is a large project which could have succumbed to gigantism. However, in its innovative spatial plan and daring palette of materials, Nokia House certainly breaks new ground.

location
espoo, finland

client
oy nokia ab

completed
march 1997

total floor space
38,600 square metres
(415,500 square feet)

staff
44 people

cost
£12 million

1 One of the two main central atria with ground floor restaurant and spiral staircases taking staff to upper levels. Extensive use of redwoods redefines the conventional 'white halls' of modern Finnish architecture.

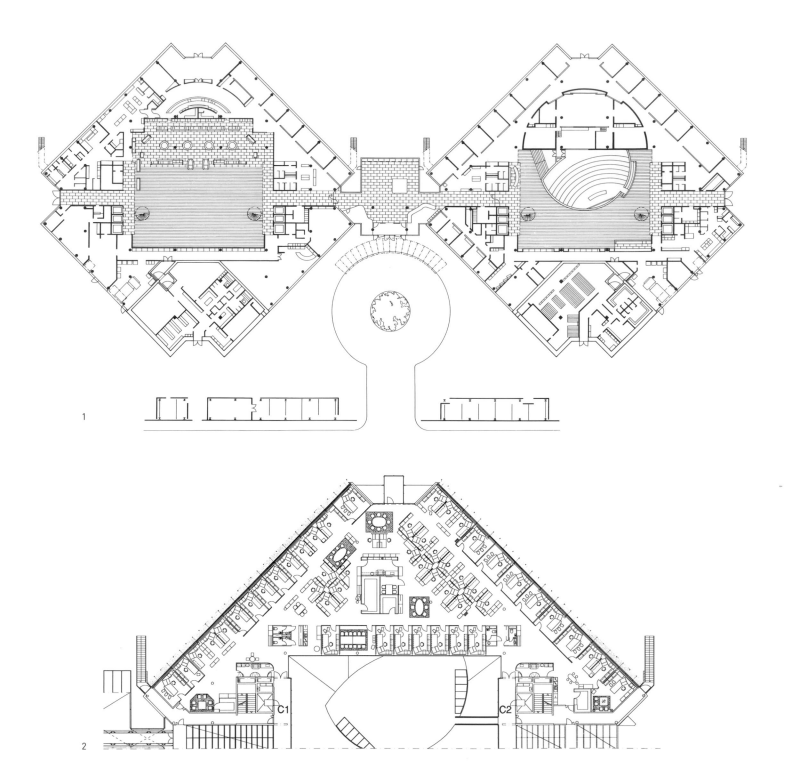

1   Ground floor plan of the building showing the twin atria.

2   Typical work area based on triangular plan, designed to accommodate
    up to 80 people in an environment that promotes 'positive encounters'.

3   View into the main atrium from a private office.

1 Ground floor seating area adjacent to meeting
   rooms. A calm and relaxed environment
   designed to make Nokia's knowledge workers
   feel creative and wanted.

2 North-west entrance façade

3 Section

2

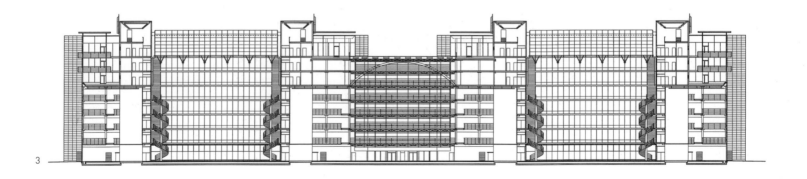

1

3

p o m e g r a n i t   HOLEY ASSOCIATES

POMEGRANIT is a post-production company based in San Francisco's 'advertising gulch' and housed in one of the few remaining landmark brick warehouses on the city's Barbary Coast waterfront. Its street level office opens directly on to a cobblestone lane, a large glazed arch affording passers-by a view into the spacious, light-industrial premises while bringing natural light into the workplace.

Indeed openness is a keynote of the scheme: the process of editing TV commercials is highly collaborative and involves many meetings with both the advertising agency and the agency's clients to discuss how best to realize creative intent. According to designers Holey Associates, the objective of the Pomegranit project was 'an open environment where information is easily shared'.

The need to make space transparent and activity visible to the entire group while also providing varying levels of client privacy dictated the plan. At its heart is the Great Hall with redwood ceilings 6 metres (20 feet) high. This space acts as a piazza and knits the project together, incorporating reception area, informal conversation area and café.

John Holey of Holey Associates says the Great Hall functions like an 'Office Home' – its amenities have a domestic scale and informality, using casually arranged sofas and tables to create a more comfortable working environment in a business where the production team talks the client through its proposed approach. Clients are encouraged to bring their children to Pomegranit and a place has been set aside for them to play computer games at terminals.

Edit suites – key elements of the scheme – are located just off the Great Hall to provide convenient client access, audio privacy and Internet connections. An office, graphics suite, video library and conference room also radiate from the hub of the Great Hall, either shielded from view by a sliding screen or open to all comers, depending on the activity of the day.

This is a scheme in which high-tech editing and graphics systems have been integrated into an industrial warehouse fabric of muted colours and utilitarian materials with the utmost skill and precision. A metal mesh and maple staircase in the centre of the piazza leads up to a mezzanine-level production area, a further facet of a creative community dedicated to exchanging ideas in a way which balances dynamism with comfort.

1 View from the street through the glazed arch north façade into Pomegranit's Great Hall.

2 Comfortable workspace reflects the idea of the 'office home': casual sofas coexist with new technology.

location
san francisco, USA

client
pomegranit

completed
march 1998

total floor space
557 square metres
(6,000 square feet)

staff
20 people

cost
undisclosed

1

1 View from the
kitchen to the Great
Hall. This robust-
looking central
piazza knits the
whole scheme
together.

1

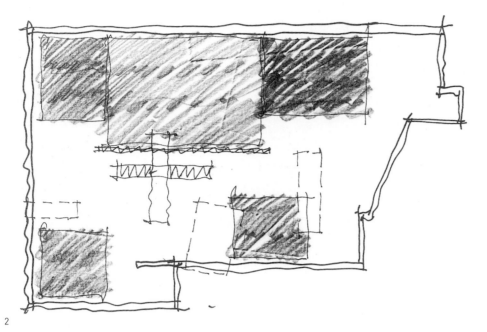

2

3

1 Canopy detail at
Pomegranit
entry/reception.

2 Concept diagram
showing division of
elements.

3 Ground floor plan

4 Mezzanine floor plan

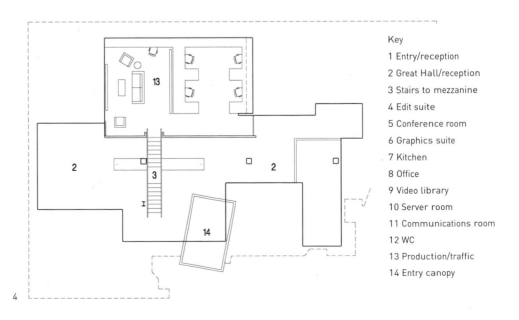

4

Key

1 Entry/reception

2 Great Hall/reception

3 Stairs to mezzanine

4 Edit suite

5 Conference room

6 Graphics suite

7 Kitchen

8 Office

9 Video library

10 Server room

11 Communications room

12 WC

13 Production/traffic

14 Entry canopy

hiratsuka bank   KUNIHIKO HAYAKAWA

AS a working environment, a bank must reconcile the needs of security, confidentiality and privacy with the desire to create a spirit of openness and exchange with new customers. This Japanese project for the Kanda branch office of a credit bank is a highly innovative solution which seeks to moderate between the closed nature and the open nature of this office type.

Architect Kunihiko Hayakawa has created a branch that not only offers the usual banking services but provides meeting and conference facilities for small local businesses in the bank's prefecture of operation.

A light and airy four-storey building constructed in glass and steel opens on to a major arterial highway in a welcoming way. Inside the structure, a large frosted glass cone appears to float within the interior volume. This suspended element contains a reception room and a meeting area. A suspended cylindrical concrete deck on the top level also provides a rest room.

An interplay between the openness of building envelope and the closed mystery of the suspended glass cone within entices the first-time visitor while maintaining a harmony between public and private functions. This is a simple scheme combining sparse finishes and minimal classic furniture. The aim in both general plan and architectural details is for maximum transparency and openness – but not at the expense of customer confidence in the confidentiality of every financial negotiation and transaction.

location
kanda, japan

client
hiratsuka bank

completed
april 1996

total floor space
692 square metres
(7,450 square feet)

staff
14 people

cost
£1.4 million

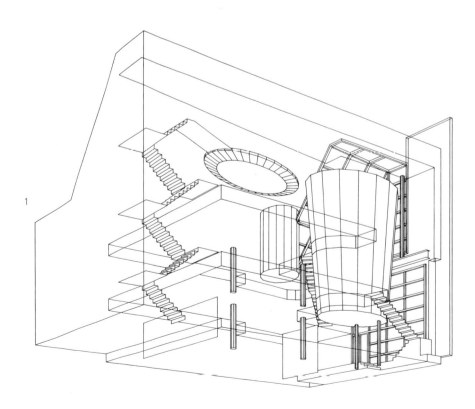

1

1 Axonometric showing how the four levels work with the glass cone suspended in the interior volume.

2 The building's openness contrasts with the closed mystery of the frosted glass element inside, creating tensions between public welcome and private transaction.

1 Calm meeting and
   rest area on fourth level
   concrete deck.

2 First floor plan

3 Second floor plan

4 Fourth floor plan

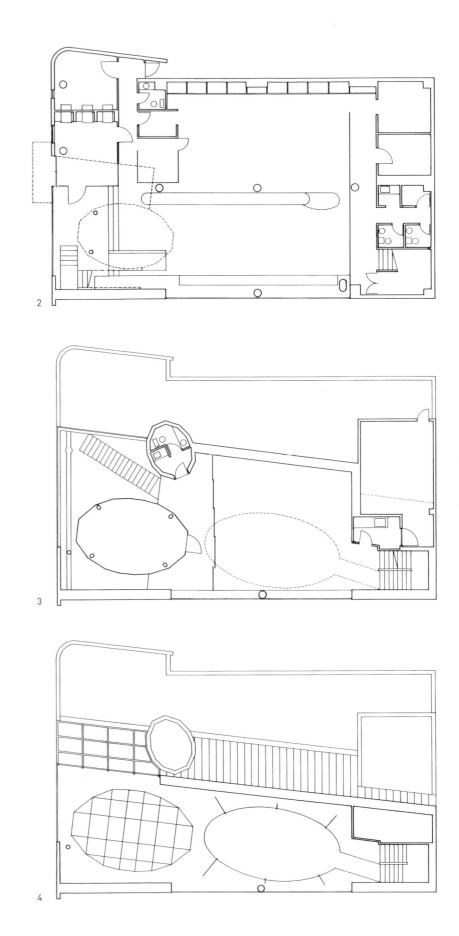

natuzzi americas MARIO BELLINI ASSOCIATI

ITALIAN architect Mario Bellini has created a signature office building in North Carolina which acts as a corporate headquarters and 'furniture market' for his client, a furniture company. Thus there are two distinct types of office space in the building, the curved glass-and-aluminium façade of which cuts through the streetscape like a ship's prow through water.

On the top floor, Natuzzi's year-round administrative engine runs in a group of cellular offices which connect to an open-plan central terrace through wide glazed walls. On the third floor below is the 'furniture market' which combines showroom with workplace in a novel way. This 'market' admits clients twice a year to view the company's latest lines and negotiate with sales agents. It is a forum to barter, banter and exchange information, and it has been conceived by Bellini as a wide open gallery criss-crossed by a series of catwalks within a strict geometric frame.

Within this grid, clients and sales staff travel around the space, inspecting the furniture and meeting up at 'attraction points'. A third-floor bar and restaurant facilitate discussion, and a series of adjacent meeting rooms then allow client negotiation to be concluded and contracts to be signed.

Bellini's idea is that the key players in this commercial exchange are like the main characters in a staged 'event'. The drama unfolds against a set of birch-panelled gallery pillars and beams, with stainless steel and glass denoting the catwalks. In fact there are showroom spaces on the first three levels of the building but only the third floor 'market' incorporates display with offices to such dramatic effect.

From the ground-floor reception, with its local rough-cut black stone flooring, to the upper showroom floors of unrolled birch and aluminium profiles, this is a scheme in which the extrovert character of Natuzzi is shown on every level. The client played a central role in the design process, including furnishing the new headquarters itself. Furniture office-showrooms are notoriously difficult to make special and glamorous, given the mundaneness of their transactions. But Bellini's meticulous interior concept – realized using local building expertise and imported materials from Treviso, Italy – is a fair attempt at adding value. Giovanna Bonfanti, Giovanni Cappelletti and Matteo Bulli worked with Bellini on the design.

location
high point,
north carolina, USA

client
natuzzi americas inc.

completed
1998

total floor space
10,000 square metres
(107,640 square feet)

staff
variable (150 maximum)

cost
$13 million

1

1   Mario Bellini's ship-like corporate headquarters for Natuzzi Americas.

2   Fabrics displayed within the grid-like gallery: this seasonal 'market' combines workplace and showroom in a novel way.

2

1

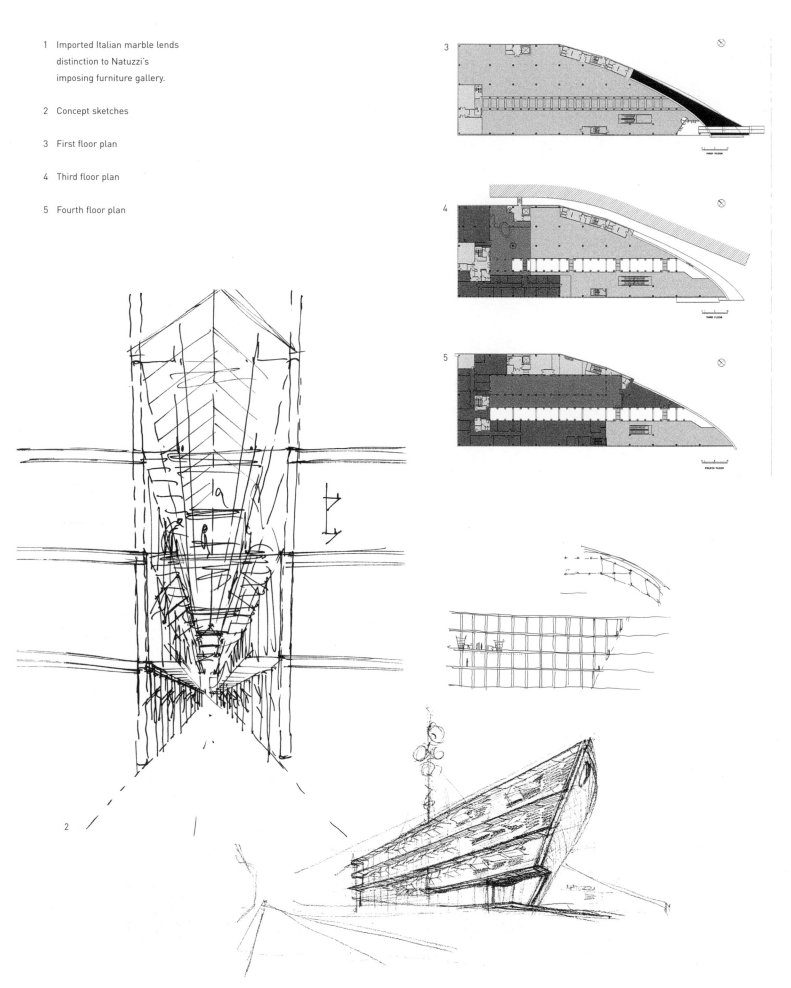

1 Imported Italian marble lends
  distinction to Natuzzi's
  imposing furniture gallery.

2 Concept sketches

3 First floor plan

4 Third floor plan

5 Fourth floor plan

IBM australia DARYL JACKSON INTERNATIONAL

THE west tower of the Southgate complex in Melbourne has been shaped by many designers. Its shell was designed by Buchan Laird and Bawden, and eight of the tower's top ten floors occupied by IBM were fitted out by Geyer Design. But the most striking and unusual design work belongs to floors 27 and 28, IBM's front-of-house marketing centre, designed by Daryl Jackson International.

This is a facility in which customers can learn how to use IBM equipment, so the interiors speak the language of exchange, instruction and interaction through a combination of sensitive planning and sensual materials.

Daryl Jackson was commissioned early enough in the tower's construction to intervene in the design of the ground floor lobby, extending its depth, reordering its elements and hinting at IBM's presence above through the sophistication of granite surface banding and a light installation. But the real quality shines through in the marketing centre on floors 27 and 28.

Here briefing rooms, seminar rooms, classrooms and ancillary space are planned in simple rectilinear patterns around the core in response to the lozenge configuration of the tower's floor plate. Corridors form a structured circulation route around both floors, with residual break-out spaces grouped on the perimeter so that clients taking a break from the hard work of briefing or instruction are immediately rewarded by magnificent views of the city, port and bay.

The sense of connection with the world outside is reinforced by the use of 'floating' translucent partitions, made of rice paper sandwiched between glass, to define the perimeter briefing rooms. These draw natural light through the space in a manner reminiscent of Japanese *shoji* screens; the total effect is one of gently being aware of activity in adjacent areas, without compromising acoustic or visual privacy. The screens are punctuated by veneered pearwood columns.

Other keynotes of the scheme include oversized doors and sliding screens which can be opened and moved to alter patterns of informal movement, and a sculptural staircase stretching from the main reception area on floor 27 to the floor above. The project's spare and elegant finishes include a ceiling of perforated metal and curved walls of aluminium, some with sliding panels. Custom-made furniture, with white laminate panels inserted into a modular aluminium frame, completes a confident scheme in which visitors to IBM and instructing staff share an interior landscape of measured intelligence and occasional delight.

location
melbourne, australia

client
IBM

completed
1994

total floor space
9,000 square metres
(96,880 square feet)

staff
variable

cost
AUS $25 million

1

1   The IBM reception area on floor 27
    opens on to a glass-and-steel staircase
    connecting to the upper customer
    service floor. Walls are veneered
    in pearwood.

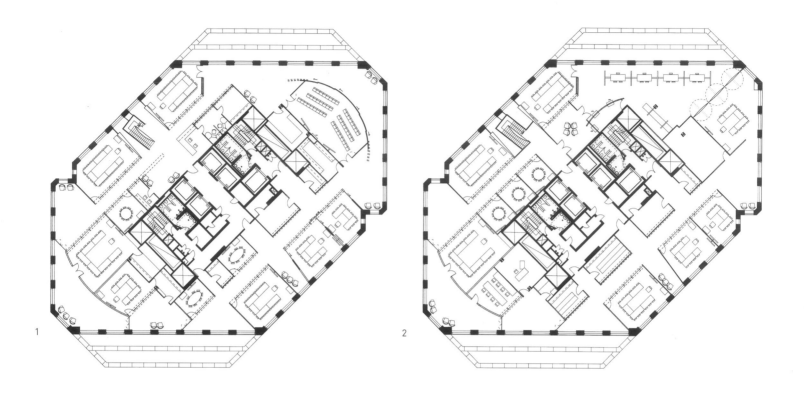

1

2

3

1 Level 27 floor plan

2 Level 28 floor plan

3 Functional demonstration
   room with Charles Eames
   seating.

4 The ground floor lobby
   has been remodelled with
   a new light installation
   as part of the project to add
   an element of sophistication
   to visiting IBM Australia.

4

independiente

JESTICO + WHILES

YOUNG and vibrant record companies can make noisy neighbours. When Andy MacDonald daringly decided that his record label, Independiente, would occupy a former drill hall on a tight west London site hemmed in on three sides by local residents, including apartment owners in an adjacent warehouse, an important consideration for designers Jestico + Whiles was sound insulation.

Initially, the demand for an office comprising a series of acoustically separated spaces appeared at odds with the single interior volume of this remarkable but rotting and neglected brick and terracotta hall. This sturdy space was held up internally by timber-laminated arched trusses, each strapped by bolted metal ties. Only three roof lights and a series of small windows on the north elevation allowed daylight into the hall, underlining the need to keep the space open to allow in as much light as possible.

MacDonald wanted to create an atmosphere of interaction and exchange between the different departments of his new company – A&R (artists and repertoire), creative, marketing, finance, legal, management and reception. But he also wanted to allow ownership of individual spaces. The design solution not only resolves the contradictions in the brief but is a powerful and elegant response to the original architectural fabric, using raw, low-cost industrial components to make a series of intelligent interventions in the interior.

At the heart of the refurbishment is a central well of double-height space up to the reconstructed and acoustically sealed roof. Informal-looking offices are grouped asymmetrically around the perimeter of the building on the ground floor and on a newly inserted mezzanine level. The central public domain of the building is bridged by the curving metallic mezzanine walkway, which is lined with open balustrading and paved with glass, light-emitting bricks.

Purpose-made sound-insulating boards and acoustic glass panels bedded on neoprene strips in welded steel frames were designed to front the offices, so that noise is contained but light falls between different spaces. The slightly eccentric space plan allows a division between public and private but never destroys the singular character of the original interior, creating an appropriately robust and youthful setting for the offices of Independiente.

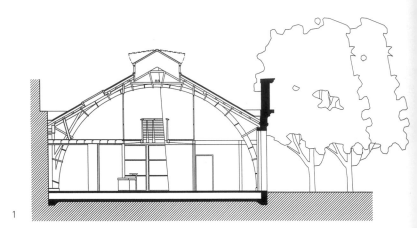

1

location
london, UK

client
independiente record company

completed
december 1997

total floor space
500 square metres
(5,380 square feet)

staff
20 people

cost
variable

1 Section showing the
   drill hall held up by
   timber arched trusses.

2 View of the custom-
   designed reception desk
   at Independiente, with
   the curved mezzanine
   walkway above acting as
   a public balcony.

2

1

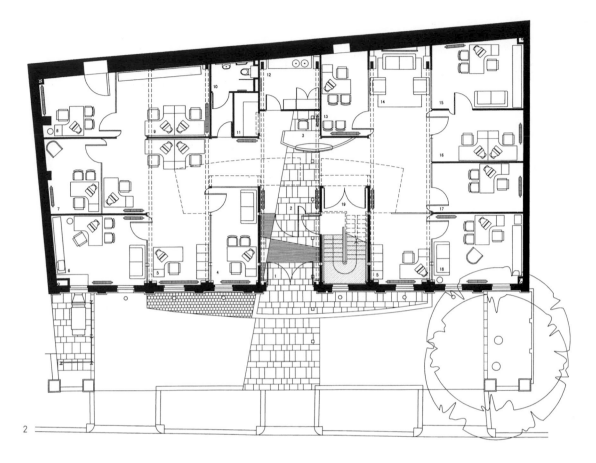

2

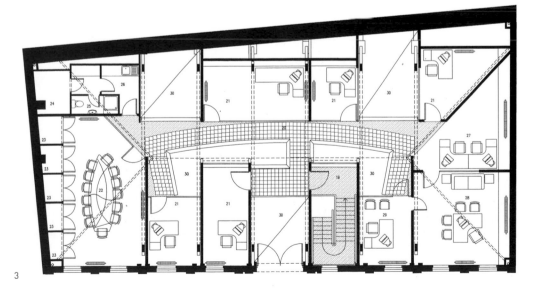

3

1 The new glazed entrance
   hints at interior
   transformation.

2 Ground floor plan

3 Mezzanine floor plan

Key
1 Outer entry
2 Entrance foyer
3 Reception
4 Marketing manager
5 Personnel assistant
6 Managing director
7 Creative director
8 Accounts manager
9 Accounts
10 WC
11 Mail room
12 Kitchen
13 Press room
14 Waiting
15 International manager
16 International staff
17 Office
18 Legal
19 Stairs
20 Glass block bridge
21 Artists & Repertoire
22 Meeting room
23 Storage
24 Plant room
25 WC/shower room
26 Kitchen
27 A&R coordinator
28 General manager
29 Personal assistant
30 Void

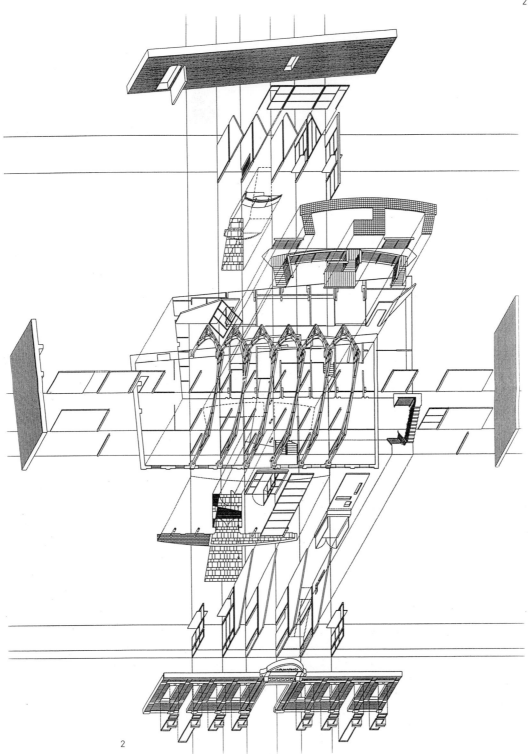

1   A glass block bridge leads
    to mezzanine-level offices
    in this independent record
    company headquarters.

2   Exploded projection takes
    apart the elements of
    the refurbished drill hall.

2

1

andersen consulting

EVA JIRICNA ARCHITECTS

PRAGUE'S Rasin Building, a speculative corner office block owned by the Nationale Nederlanden Bank and nicknamed 'Fred and Ginger', is no shrinking violet on its prestigious site. Its proximity to local nineteenth-century architectural landmarks and views along the Vltava River towards the green hill of Petrin and Prague's famous Castle complex encouraged its designers Frank Gehry and Vlado Milunic to abandon restraint and build a controversial 'dancing tower'.

Externally, the Rasin Building has a pronounced irregular curve shape which changes the arrangement of different levels and almost dares tenants to work with the internal office space. But for Andersen Consulting, the global management consultants renowned for pioneering innovation in work style, this challenge was no deterrent.

Requiring a new Eastern European headquarters and a focus for its training facilities in the region, Andersen Consulting chose to occupy three of the five available floors within the building. The interior scheme, designed by Eva Jiricna Architects with Prague-based Architectural Associates, cleverly accommodates the operational needs of a demanding client without diminishing the bold character of Gehry and Milunic's signature architecture.

This balancing act is achieved chiefly by extensive use of glass partitions which allow continual interior views of the building's curved façade. It is an approach that underlines the openness of a non-territorial scheme in which at least one-third of the workspace is given over to hot-desking – project consultants working mainly off site are not allocated a personal workstation but simply reserve space for the time they need it.

The brief specified a range of conference, meeting and projection rooms, as well as a lower floor training centre, in an organization dedicated to an open exchange of ideas and information. To achieve this, the ceiling was realigned at different heights, to take fluorescent uplighting, low-voltage downlighting and air-conditioning grilles.

Conference furniture and work desks, custom designed and fabricated in France using stained maple, powder-coated metal and glass, further promote the sense of egalitarian calm that permeates the environment. The cable distribution network running through the floor circulates through the desks, via a flap at worktop level. Storage is arranged in centralized cupboard units. Andersen Consulting's worldwide standards were difficult to achieve given local conditions in the Czech Republic, but this is a project that conforms to best practice while never losing its special sense of place.

1

location
prague,
czech republic

client
andersen consulting

completed
1996

total floor space
1,250 square metres
(13,500 square feet)

staff
55 people

cost
undisclosed

2

1 Gehry and Milunic's controversial 'Fred and Ginger' building in Prague: a challenge to any office tenant.

2 Interior view shows how glass panels expose the building's continuous irregular 'dancing' façade.

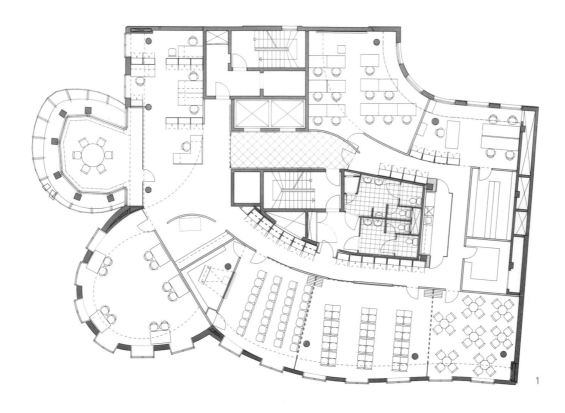

1

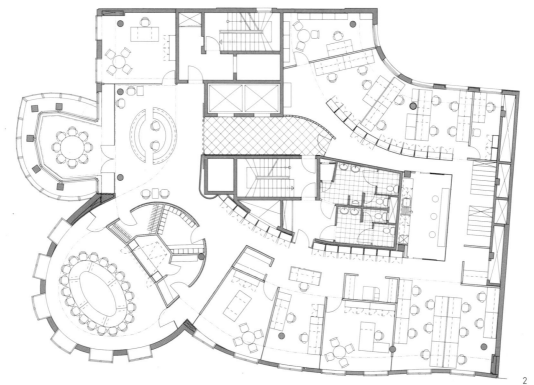

2

3

1 Sixth floor plan

2 Seventh floor plan

3 Conference room, achieving a lightness of approach through
the use of glass and subtle lighting effects.

seghers engineering   **SAMYN AND PARTNERS**

THIS office for a Belgian firm of engineers creates a modern, minimalist, rigorously precise working environment within an unusual historic building, the Lamot Brewery, originally constructed in 1837 and added to in various ways until 1911. Since 1950, the brewery has been closed, so the task for architects Samyn and Partners was to convert this redundant industrial structure into the type of professional office where ideas and information could be readily exchanged.

The Lamot Brewery building consists of six interconnecting parallelepidec volumes of varying dimensions and degrees of regularity, grouped in a loose U shape around a courtyard. The first volume contains five levels and is linked on its western frontage to a second, less regular volume containing four levels.

The central volume is a rectangular-shaped kiln topped with a magnificent cylindrical chimney. Restoration was begun late in 1998 on the north wing, the brewer's house, left untouched in the first phase of the project.

1

The architects set about the structural repair of the building, putting in new foundations and concrete floors where necessary, replacing cracked masonry brick by brick, and retaining the external appearance except for new wooden window frames inserted flush to the walls and painted grey. They then explored how to maximize social circulation.

The locations of stairways are intended to allow natural light into a maximum number of workplaces. This led to the decision to build a narrow atrium between two volumes, complete with steel spiral staircase and glazed elevator. A main concrete staircase lined with wood prolongs the atrium space between volumes up to glass roof terraces – which themselves provide further unusual and engaging work settings. The atrium allows for windows to be regularly spaced with workstations right across this zone.

All data cabling and servicing runs around the workplace in the void between the concrete floor slabs and new hardwood strip flooring. Private offices are created by fitting laminated transparent glass panels flush with floors and ceiling. Solid wooden doors provide access to these areas. A compact furniture system was custom-designed by the architects for the building, based on a modular approach incorporating sliding panels and integrated indirect-fluorescent light fittings. With the emphasis on energy saving, fluorescent lighting is used in work areas, WCs and circulation areas. Only the atrium features halogen lighting.

Simple and direct, this scheme has breathed fresh life into an empty brewery complex in a measured and practical way entirely in keeping with its purpose as a base for engineers.

location
klein willebroek, belgium

client
seghers engineering

completed
february 1997

total floor space
2,225 square metres
(23,950 square feet)

staff
115 people

cost
undisclosed

1   External view of the Lamot Brewery.

2   A dramatic spiral staircase threads up the narrow glazed atrium between two refurbished volumes.

2

1 Natural light penetrates a sparse,
  functional meeting area.

2 Plan showing the five major
  refurbished volumes of the
  project, plus sixth (shaded right) –
  the brewer's house – the
  conversion of which was begun
  in a later phase.

3 Glazed roof terracing:
  extending the workplace with
  an economy of means.

1

3

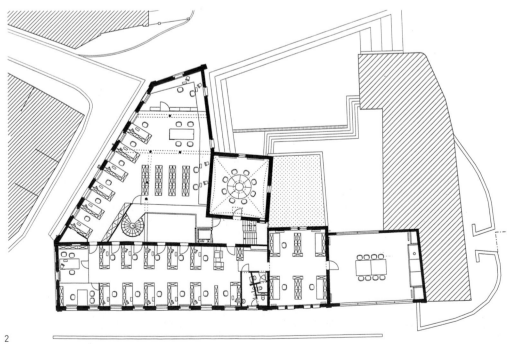

2

lowe and partners/sms SEDLEY PLACE

THE tension between the individual and the organization is never more apparent than in a global advertising agency where the needs of corporate professionalism and consistency must be balanced against the personal motivations and whims of the agency's planners, art directors and copywriters.

This scheme by London-based designers Sedley Place is for a New York agency, owned by the Interpublic Group, on five floors of the WR Grace Building, a 1970s Manhattan high-rise on Sixth Avenue. It presents an expressive, Art Deco-tinged environment in which agency staff can create work settings which respond to personal tastes and needs within an overall design that remains reassuringly constant.

To achieve this difficult objective, the designers brought a high level of technical innovation to the project. Centrepiece of the scheme is a magnificent metal-and-teak staircase, inserted into a stairwell punching through the slabs of floors 19, 20 and 21 of the building. This feature improves horizontal and vertical communication, creating the agency's communal heart. A huge, backlit stained-glass work of art by Brian Clarke, entitled Chelsea Window, illuminates the stairwell.

The plan then develops on conventional lines with rows of cellular offices – although the coveted corner areas of the building are devoted to common areas rather than office space for senior managers, and the flooring is a spectacular assemblage of imported materials, including English slate, Italian marble and limestone from Israel. At strategic points along routes, TV monitors sunken into the flooring emit light and a sense of movement. This is a project with constant flashes of wit and decorative detail. Even the bathrooms make bold play on materials.

Within the cellular offices, a series of custom elements provide maximum flexibility for the individual. A low-energy lighting system based on sensors responding to the heat and movement of the user is incorporated into movable light fixtures. Each office has a custom-made skirting and door frame system to take concealed cable management around the perimeter. Custom-designed office wall display panels, which slot into aluminium channels at base and ceiling level, allow work to be held neatly to surfaces by magnets.

A special system of tables and desks, designed by Sedley Place and composed of triangular, square and trapezoidal units in different finishes which just butt together, allows occupants to create their own furniture combination without outside help. Customization of this kind means that the scheme responds fluently to the individual while never forgetting the overall corporate image.

1 Interior view reflects the Art Deco inspiration behind this Manhattan advertising agency office. Doorways have veneered inlays; marble, slate and even television screens are set into limestone floors.

location
new york, USA

client
lowe and partners/sms

completed
march 1998

total floor space
15,000 square metres
(161,460 square feet)

staff
500 people

cost
undisclosed

1

1   The magnificent
    decorative staircase
    that unites three floors
    of the agency, improving
    both vertical and
    horizontal circulation.

2   Stair treads are of teak
    with various wood inlays.

1

2

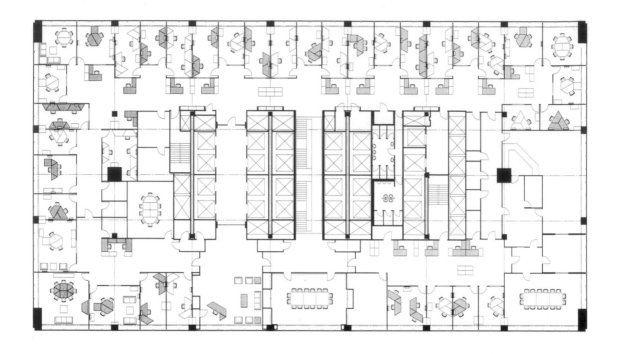

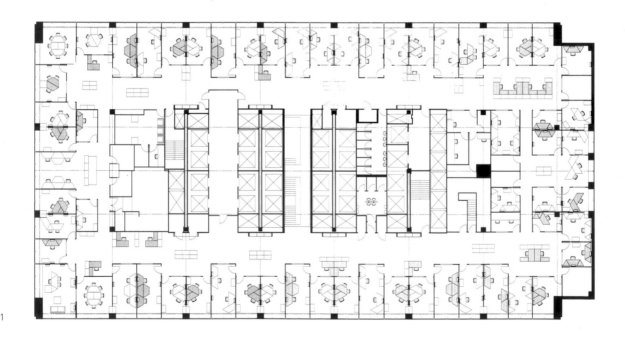

2

1

3

1   20th and 21st floor plans

2   Bathrooms extend
    the Art Deco period
    flavour, with slate floors
    and ribbed cherrywood
    vanity cabinets.

3   Private office allowing
    extensive individual
    customization. The
    furniture with butting
    triangular units can be
    easily reconfigured;
    lights can be slid into
    new positions; metal wall
    display panels hold
    notices with magnets.

rover design and engineering centre

WEEDON PARTNERSHIP

IN response to intense levels of competition in the car industry, British car maker Rover decided to centralize all its design studio and project engineering facilities in one building. The new design centre is intended to dramatically reduce the lead time from concept to manufacture in the development of new models.

Architect Terry Lee of the Weedon Partnership studied the work patterns of Rover designers and engineers in order to understand the way they wanted to share knowledge and information during the development of new cars in the future. The resulting building on the company's 364 hectare (900 acre) testing site in Warwickshire is a spectacular testament to this collaborative approach: it not only unites all of Rover's designers and engineers under one roof for the first time but also reflects the company's brand heritage, which includes the Rover, Land Rover and MG marques.

The light and airy centre is laid out around an internal street running east to west, the street width determined by the need to move large, unpowered vehicles from the workshops to other parts of the complex. At the west end of the street, which incorporates a café and informal meeting areas, are the high-security design facilities, including the main studio and colour and trim studio. North of the spectacular reception area four storeys high is a block containing directors' workspace and boardroom on the top floor, two floors of project team space for 650 engineers and a ground floor network of meeting rooms used by all divisions of the Rover Group. There is also a showroom overlooking an internal viewing courtyard.

The main open-plan office areas are bright and spacious with views of the surrounding countryside. Vehicle parts and whole vehicles are on prominent display, reflecting an intimacy between people, process and product. A key aspect of the project was the development of a £1 million custom furniture range specifically for use in the building, designed and made by UK manufacturer Project. This range has a series of dockable parts to provide the team space planning flexibility required.

Everyone in the building works in open plan except for the managing director and design studio director. It is a tribute to the interdisciplinary and user-focused way in which the centre was developed that a car development process requiring such high levels of security and secrecy can be undertaken in such an open and appealing environment.

location
gaydon, warwickshire, UK

client
rover group

completed
october 1996

total floor space
30,380 square metres
(327,000 square feet)

interior design consultant
alison montieth

staff
1,500 people

cost
£29.3 million

1

2

1   Two tiers of open-plan
    project team space
    for Rover's engineers:
    the furniture was
    custom designed for
    the company.

2   A view along the centre's
    internal street, designed
    to promote interaction.

1 Ground floor plan

2 Section

3 The internal street, wide
   enough to take unpowered
   vehicles to and from the
   workshops, has a café and
   informal meeting areas.
   It provides the facility's
   creative heart.

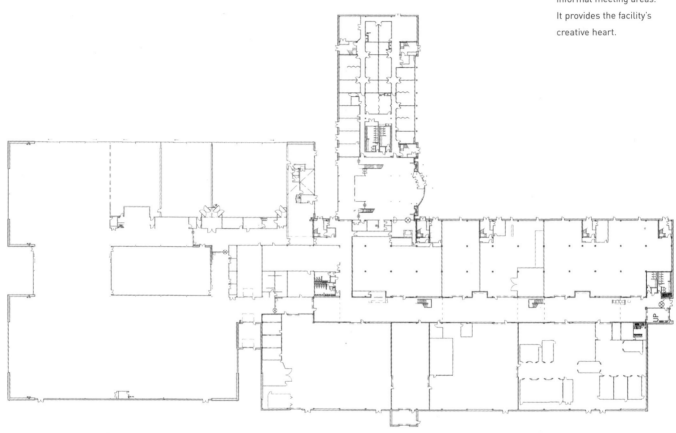

1

2

3

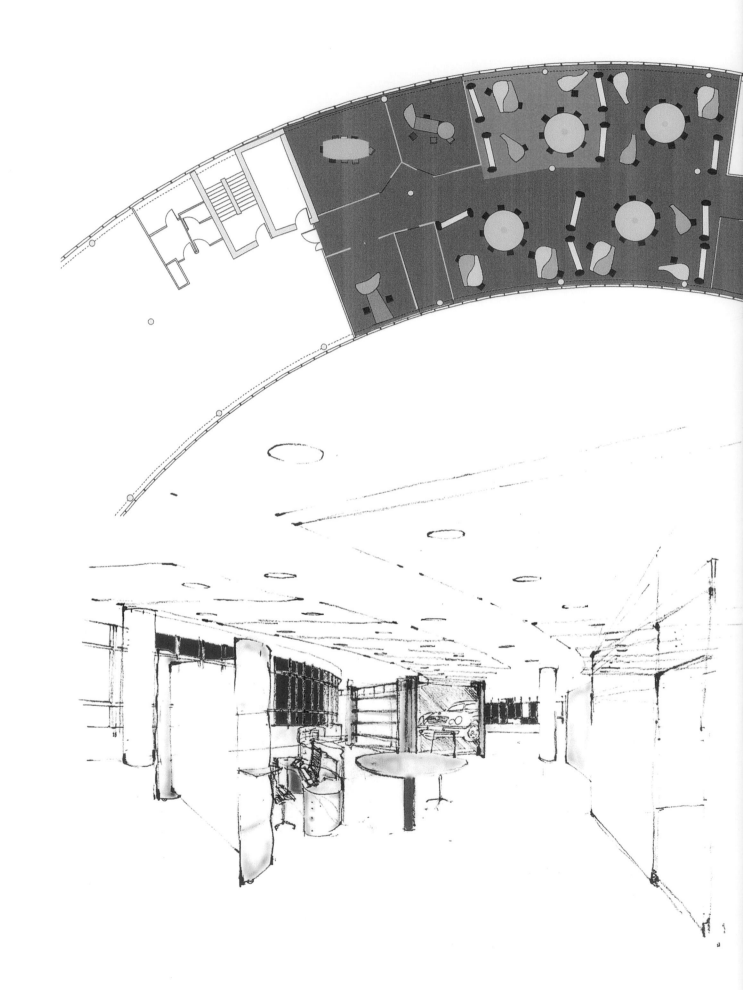

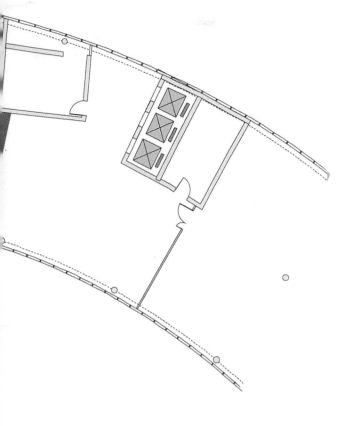

automotive industry office
MAHMOUDIEH DESIGN

THIS 'exchange office' concept was developed by Mahmoudieh Design for the offices of a major German car manufacturer.

The design brings people out of cellular offices into open-plan team space that provides a legible area for six to eight people. Within each area users are provided with a choice of environment that allows them to work either in a standing or seated position at adjustable desks or at a central shared round table.

The team is given privacy by the placing of a 'wardrobe' at each end of the space; a flexible piece of furniture that has storage on one side and a versatile writing or projection surface on the other. All people within the space are equipped with pocket office telephones allowing complete flexibility. For privacy, users can go to one of a series of 'think cells' where they can make a telephone call or just work alone.

Shown here is a plan of the space and interior view with concept sketches for flexible furniture (below).

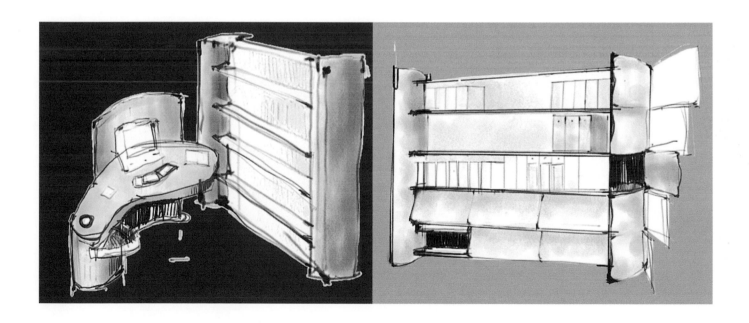

OFFICES were once rooted in a work ethic in which conviviality and comfort had no place. Workplaces were functional and impersonal and frowned on social contact. But in the creative office, there is growing recognition that work has a social dynamic which is productive and valuable. Old-fashioned adjacencies are replaced by a new approach to office interiors, in which the

comm

buzz and colour of real city life is simulated by the design of neighbourhoods and piazzas, cafés and boulevards as spaces in which to work. The compact communities and good neighbours that result from such thinking frequently produce more creative and collaborative work styles. The following selection of office schemes demonstrates the concept of community.

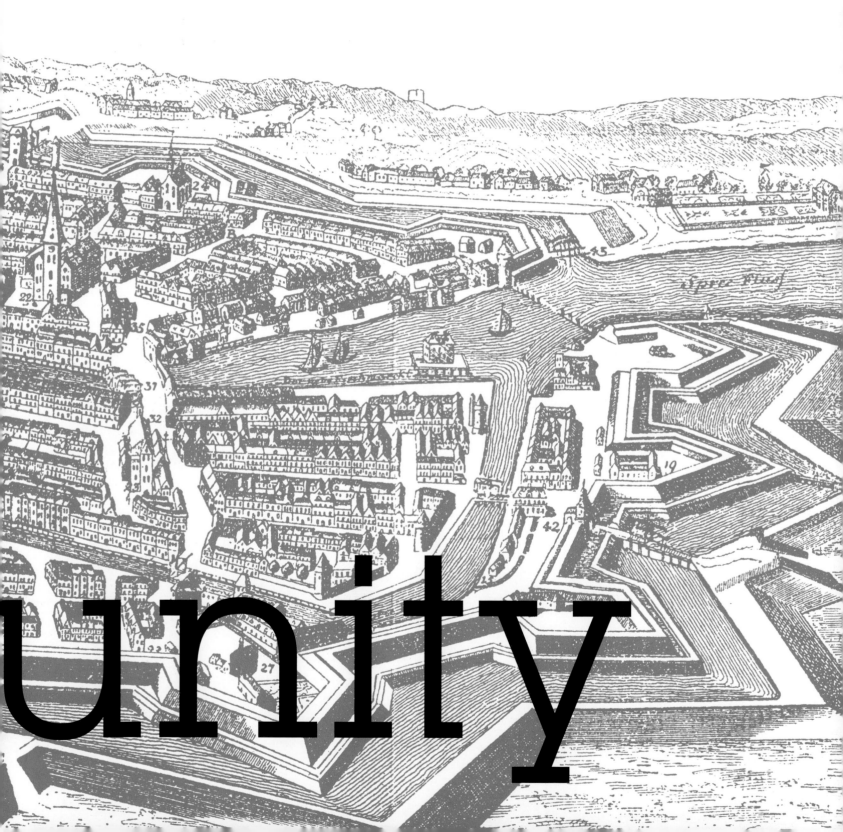

unity

nortel brampton centre

HELLMUTH, OBATA + KASSABAUM

BY converting a digital switching factory built in 1963, telecommunications company Nortel has created an unusual and highly appropriate setting for its worldwide headquarters. The scale of the old manufacturing site required the architect, HOK, to manage both volume and orientation – a 'city planning' approach was adopted to break down the scale of the old factory and create a new sense of community.

The space has been divided into areas based around 'neighbourhoods'; each has conference facilities, privacy nodes and a special space such as a war room (in which to plan competitive strategies) or lounge area. These neighbourhoods provide people with a choice of work settings and in effect the 'citizens' are free to design their own local work environment. Some have chosen the 'cube'; others have created more chaotic, process-driven spaces. This adaptable approach has had the effect of producing a diverse and dynamic environment that responds to the changing needs of the community it houses.

The workstations themselves seem almost incidental, in an environment designed to bring people together and encourage continuous movement and interaction. Clear, colour-coded street signs and overhead banners help orientation and define interesting journeys through the space, such as the 'Short Circuit'. The environment encourages people to stretch themselves, take risks and learn constantly.

Materials have been used to good effect to differentiate areas: 'key access streets' have been surfaced in concrete and stone, while 'side streets and alley ways' are covered in vinyl. This demarcation extends to other aspects of the fit out, where walls of 'public buildings' (such as conference or food amenities) have been constructed using concrete while the office areas have walls made from traditional gypsum board.

The factory origins of the building have not been disguised, and a curved glass wall has been superimposed over the old factory façade. The architect built on the visual landmarks of the factory environment, and the interior reflects an industrial heritage with bold use of colour in solid blocks and exposed structural ceiling grids. Without the usual voids in which to hide technology and services, utilities have been left exposed, carried to the work areas on open trellis structures that line the main streets.

It is evident that at Brampton, the architect has created an environment in which the community not only owns the space but has adapted and improved it since moving in. The 'inhabitants' understand the city and change it according to their needs.

location
toronto, canada

client
northern telecom

completed
december 1996

total floor space
55,740 square metres
(600,000 square feet)

staff
3,000 people

cost
$50 million

1   Main street at Nortel's headquarters reflects
    the 'city planning' approach with façades of buildings
    and directional signs.

Perception Point

People Place

Colonnade

BB32

EXIT

Court

1 Staff can adapt their local
   environment and create a
   space that suits their work
   process, such as the highly
   flexible team-based space
   shown here.

2 The main entrance showing
   the new glass wall
   superimposed over the old
   factory façade.

1

2

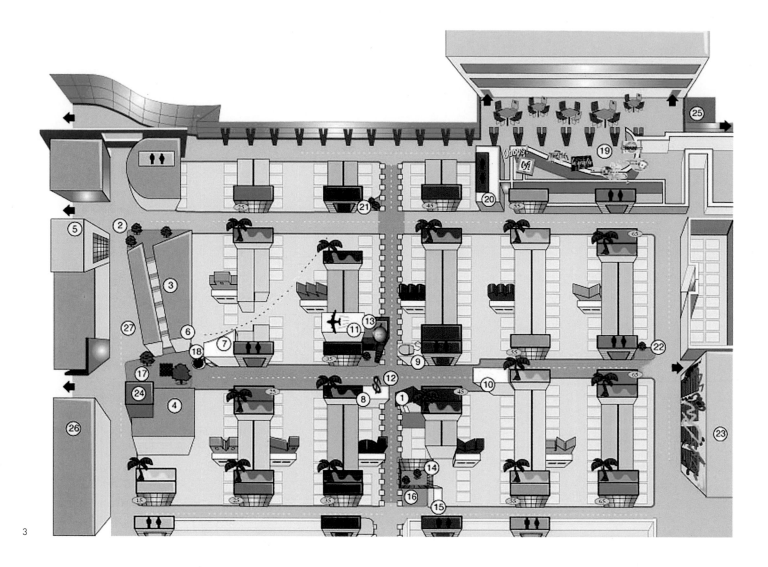

3 Floor plan showing neighbourhoods and urban planning metaphor.

1 Homebase	16 People place
2 Partnership hall	17 Venture park
3 The Interchange	18 @java.cup (coffee point)
4 Health centre	19 Courtyard
5 Business centre	20 Nortel Credit Union
6 Internet café	21 Perception point
7 Library	22 Creativity corners
8 Financial centre	23 The docklands
9 Cybershop	24 Emergency management
10 The store	centre
11 Travel agency	25 Terrace
12 Network plaza	26 Powerhouse
13 The satellite dish	27 Commerce plaza
14 Reflections (Zen garden)	
15 People's café	

2

1

1 Exposed services and
   overhead distribution of
   power and data cabling
   maintain an industrial
   feel. Coloured banners
   are used to break
   up the space and aid
   orientation.

2 The Internet café is one
   of a number of amenities
   and shared facilities that
   are scattered throughout
   this creative workplace.

ministry of defence

PERCY THOMAS PARTNERSHIP

1

STAFF at the Ministry of Defence Procurement Executive are responsible for buying all equipment for the British Armed Forces, from field radios to fighter planes. Traditionally buyers were dispersed at different locations and belonged to different branches of the Armed Forces. But the new Abbey Wood work campus is a spectacular piece of social engineering, uniting 4,400 Procurement Executive staff from 15 different offices in London, Bath, Portland and Portsmouth on a single 39 hectare (98 acre) site just outside Bristol. Eventually the office population at Abbey Wood will exceed 6,000.

Abbey Wood marks the largest relocation exercise ever undertaken by a British Government department. It reflects a process known as 'purpling' whereby Procurement Executive staff who had once solely served the army, navy or airforce would come together within a single organization. Building a sense of community and cohesion was therefore an essential part of the project.

Locals initially feared the building of a monster defence base, a 'Pentagon of the West'. But architects Percy Thomas Partnership have sensibly designed the huge campus around the concept of a 'green village' lying low in the woodlands and surrounded, not by barbed wire, but by an artificial lake for security. Abbey Wood has 13 energy-efficient buildings clustered in four neighbourhoods, all four storeys or less in height. Each neighbourhood has a covered 'street', meeting rooms and its own catering facilities.

Within the plan of a pleasant, open landscaped complex, there are piazzas, cafés, internal glazed streets, water features, a fitness centre, a nursery, an international conference centre and a circular drum library in the tradition of Asplund or Aalto. Indeed much of the design inspiration at Abbey Wood comes from Scandinavian buildings, especially the work of Niels Torp. There is also space for 3,500 cars and links to a local cycle network.

In total, Abbey Wood has 120,770 square metres (1.3 million square feet) of office space designed to improve project team integration, which has controversially taken many senior civil servants into open plan for the first time. By creating a more open community, the scheme redefines the British public sector workplace.

location
abbey wood, bristol, UK

client
ministry of defence
procurement executive

completed
june 1996

interiors designers
ptp seward

strategic planners
DEGW

total floor space
120,770 square metres
(1.3 million square feet)

staff
4,400 people

cost
£254 million

2

1 Sensitive landscaping plays a key role in the approaches to the Abbey Wood office buildings, which are reached via bridges across a security lake.

2 Master plan shows the clustering of four 'work neighbourhoods' on a green site in which more than 5,000 trees have been planted. The campus is a vehicle-free area, with car parking mainly located to the north and south.

3 Neighbourhood meeting area reflects a recognizable Scandinavian design aesthetic.

3

1 Open-plan office space,
using the same Herman
Miller workstation
for every level of the
organization.

2 Standard neighbourhood
floor plan. Planning is
based on a typical group of
50 people in an open-plan
space; three groups form a
typical 150-person floor
plan and four floors form
a typical building. A group
of three buildings then
constitute a
neighbourhood, linked
by an internal 'street'.

3 Upper level of internal
street creates a setting for
random encounters
and informal meetings.

1

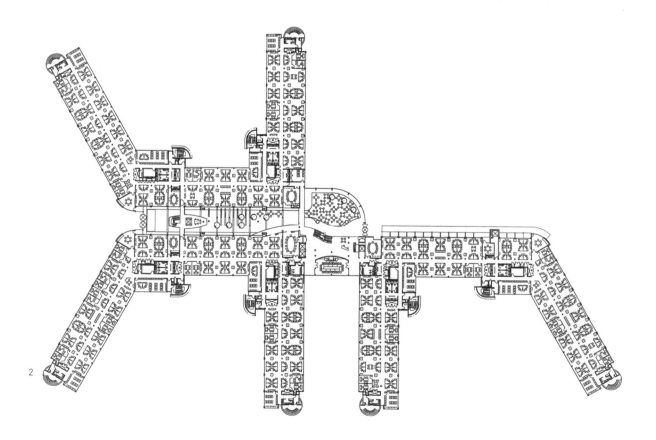

2

3

3com STUDIOS ARCHITECTURE

3Com is an American manufacturer of networking products. Its new headquarters was intended to improve time to market with new products and to resolve a range of manufacturing and quality issues. Thus this became a workplace project where there was a need to investigate adjacencies between office-based employees and those on the factory floor so that closer interaction and a stronger sense of community could emerge.

To give a sense of place in what is essentially a production facility, the designers created an open plaza or 'town centre' that provides a central square between the buildings that house manufacturing, research and development, training, customer support and a briefing centre. People are encouraged to flow through this common area, where a staff restaurant and outdoor seating is located together with landscaped public spaces.

The intentional blurring of the spatial boundaries between manufacturing and offices creates a collaborative culture. This is reinforced by physical spaces such as the 'town hall', a place where shared facilities are located and general meetings are held. Within the workplace, teaming concepts have been introduced; these are based around neighbourhoods where everyone works in open plan. The environment is varied, providing a combination of cubicles and informal meeting areas with soft seating and white boards.

In a large-scale complex, it is important to create human scale. This was achieved by locating the places where people meet at the perimeter instead of burying them deep within the buildings. According to designers Studios Architecture, the concept was to 'cloak or camouflage the manufacturing box' with human elements around its edge. This juxtaposition is reflected in the design aesthetic where the transition to office areas is almost incidental within an overtly industrial space that has exposed services and high, unenclosed ceilings.

Due emphasis has been given to the product development and manufacturing process, presenting an unobstructed open space for the advanced just-in-time plant. But staff amenities and facilities, located at the perimeter of buildings in 'clip-on' units, encourage chance meetings. The architects have intentionally designed spaces to draw staff together into informal encounters, using open stairs and corridors to break down the departmental mentality that had previously inhibited collaboration at 3Com.

location
santa clara, USA

client
3com corporation

completed
1997

total floor space
38,270 square metres
(411,950 square feet)

staff
1,400 people

cost
undisclosed

1 The 'town centre'
is an open space
that connects the
various buildings
together and
provides a place
for informal
meetings in good
weather.

1

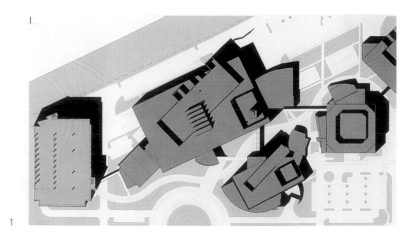

3

1 Site plan showing the five buildings in the 3Com work community.

2 Main café and restaurant looking out on to the town square. This environment stimulates collaboration between manufacturing and office-based staff by providing one place for everyone to come together for lunch or coffee breaks.

3 The open environment promotes communication and allows everyone to see the products and services being delivered, such as this network control room viewed through full height glazed partitioning.

1 Axonometric of first floor

2 First floor plan

3 Second floor plan

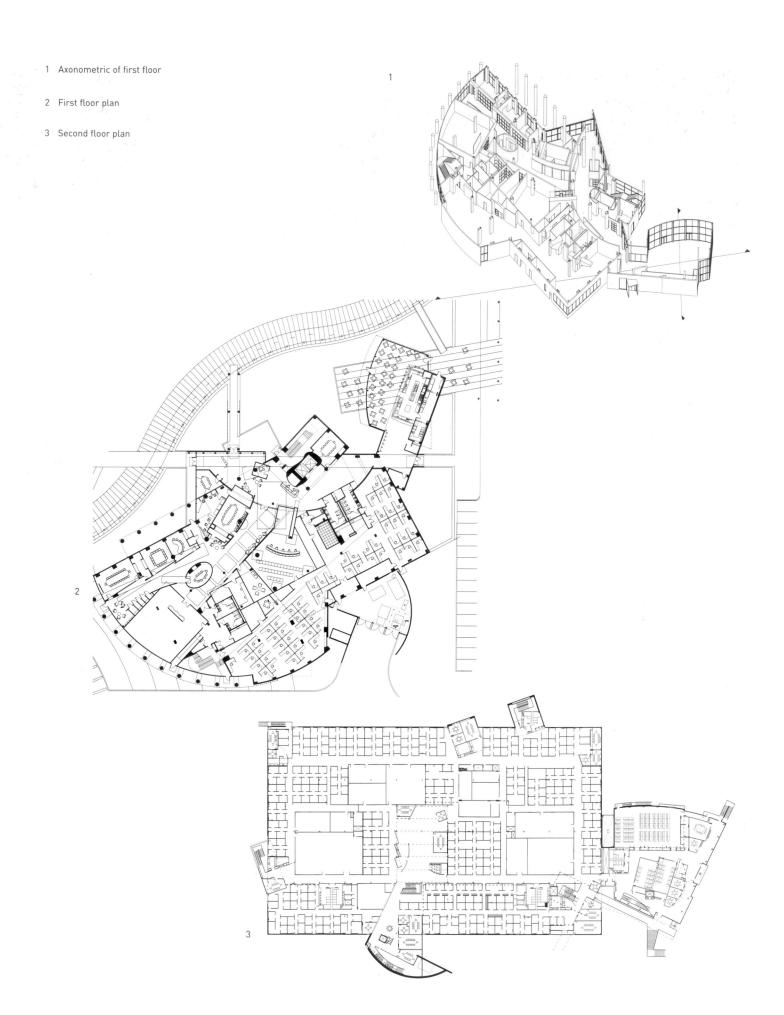

4 Informal neighbourhood area designed to stimulate
interaction between people and promote
the 'teaming' concept that has been developed to
encourage staff to work together.

commerzbank   SIR NORMAN FOSTER AND PARTNERS

'GARDEN building' is a descriptor for this unusual office, which has been designed to provide a flexible environment on a human scale, by vertical repetition through the 60 floors of what is the tallest building in Europe. The legible workspace – with access to gardens where a cool breeze and views across the city provide a contrasting environment to the office accommodation – is unexpected, certainly 210 metres (700 feet) above the streets of Frankfurt.

Designed by Sir Norman Foster and Partners, the building for Commerzbank, one of Germany's leading financial institutions, has not just set new standards in architecture but has reinvented the skyscraper as a place for real workplace innovation. Rather than endless volumes of office floors with a traditional core at the centre, this tower breaks the rules with its triangular grid, corner cores, a hollow central space and nine punctuating gardens.

These gardens are immediately striking, standing four stories high at each turn of the tower, giving the impression that they spiral upwards. They are planted according to their orientation, so the south-facing spaces have Mediterranean trees, the west-facing American grasses and the east-facing a range of bamboo and magnolia. Each garden is a visual and social focus, creating a sense of community for the 150 or so people who inhabit the surrounding floors, providing a familiar village environment for informal meetings, chance encounters, coffee, lunch or private thought.

The environmental credentials of the building are impressive and innovative. Natural ventilation has been combined with air-conditioning through a complex computerized building management system that automatically closes the windows throughout the tower and controls the microclimates for each garden.

The workspaces were compromised during the planning process, moving from a 'kombi-Büro' concept to a reality that is more conventionally cellular. However, even the workspaces provide people with unobstructed views and all offices have direct sunlight. Floor-to-ceiling glass creates a transparent workplace.

The lower floors provide public spaces, combining the building's lobby with a plaza to create a venue for the people of Frankfurt. Here a dramatic restaurant and café area has been designed by Alfredo Arribas where customers and tourists mix with staff to create a cosmopolitan atmosphere and reinforce the notion of community.

location
frankfurt, germany

client
commerzbank ag

completed
1997

total floor space
100,000 square metres
(1,076,425 square feet)

staff
2,300 people

cost
undisclosed

1 The garden provides a sense of community for the four adjacent office floors, bringing people together into this central space for meetings, lunch or informal chance encounters.

2 The building at dusk showing the gardens that punctuate the space.

3 All workstations have been planned to provide a view, either over Frankfurt or into one of the gardens, and maximize sight lines to enhance communication.

1

2

3

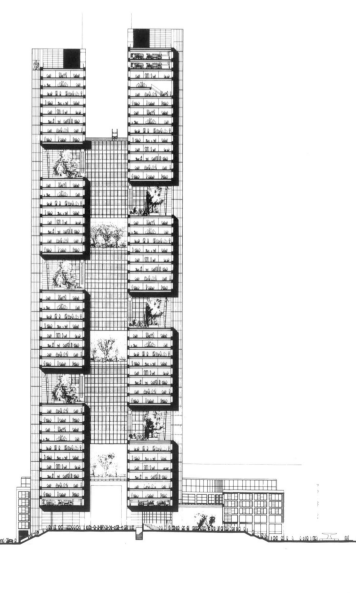

1 Each garden in the sky has been planted according to its
orientation providing different landscapes through the building.

2 Section of the Commerzbank building.

3 The dramatic ground floor restaurant has been designed by
Alfredo Arribas, allowing members of the public and tourists to mix
with staff, creating a cosmopolitan atmosphere that reinforces
the notion of community.

1 Floor plan showing
juxtaposition of the
garden with work
stations that combine
private and open-plan
spaces inspired by the
'kombi-Büro' concept.

2 The central atrium
space is left as a void
that provides natural
ventilation as opposed
to being used as a
central services core.

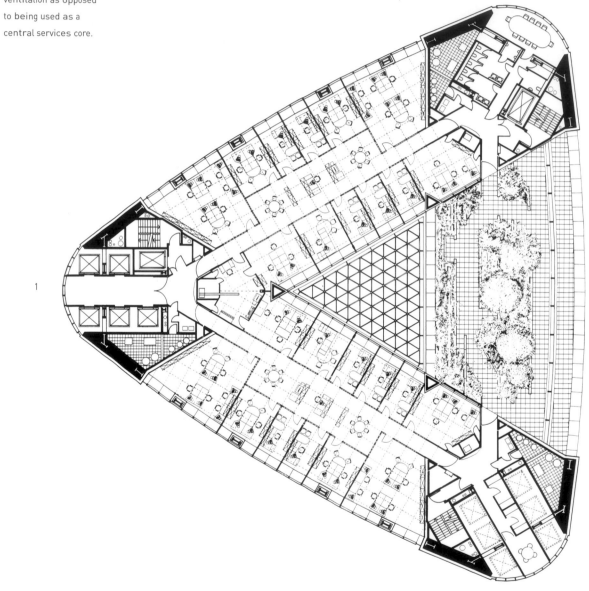

1

2

mcdonald's helsinki

HEIKKINEN-KOMONEN ARCHITECTS

WHEN compared with the banality of most McDonald's architecture, this Finnish headquarters building stands out as a strong design statement, harking back to the 1950s when Stanley Meston originally designed the first McDonald's restaurant buildings that have now become synonymous with fast food worldwide. This project was designed to provide offices and a training centre as well as a hamburger restaurant. Accordingly, it combines the need for high street consumer branding with an effective workplace for staff.

With its cylindrical design, evocations of the hamburger are obvious. Yet Heikkinen-Komonen Architects say they set out to build a structure that resembles a 'corner tower in an imaginary town wall', describing the building's position on the south-western edge of Helsinki's urban centre.

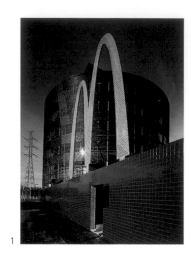

1

The striking façade is defined by a complex array of materials and layers, made from greenish glass and matt-finished aluminium sheeting. A wooden trellis that has been fastened on to the steel structure to provide a sun screen has effectively wrapped the south-facing side of the building. With its environmental concern, the flat roof has been covered with crushed recycled glass, rather than traditional roofing.

While the exterior is cylindrical, the interior reverts to a rectangular grid, presenting bright open environments that make the most of the building's transparency. Full height glazed partitions with sliding doors provide a limited demarcation between circulation and semi-enclosed team areas. Custom-designed furniture was commissioned for each area, using steel and wood to reflect the external structure.

The architects have achieved the desire for vibrancy, translucency and panorama, with an exterior view from all parts of the building and a play on materials and shapes that creates a constant sense of movement as lighting changes from daytime to night-time illumination. This is dramatized by a glazed blue 'noise wall' that supports a 6 metre (20 foot) high M logo, the 'shadow' of which has been drawn on to a wooden trellis.

With its requisite golden arches, McDonald's has long been expert at branding through architecture. This building conforms to that culture in a way that is fresh and innovative, and which provides a quality workplace.

location
helsinki, finland

client
mcdonald's

completed
october 1997

total floor space
3,580 square metres
(38,540 square feet)

workplaces
95

cost
£5.7 million

1 The dramatic yellow perforated 'golden arches' logo sits above a blue 'noise wall' that provides soundproofing and a dramatic entrance.

2 The main restaurant with its striking sculpture by Kari Cavén: *The Flight of a Bat*.

2

1 The open-plan
workstations are located
at the perimeter
of the circular building.

2 Ground floor plan
showing the restaurant
and training centre.

3 Typical office layout

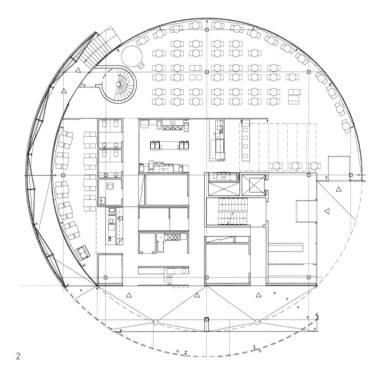

2

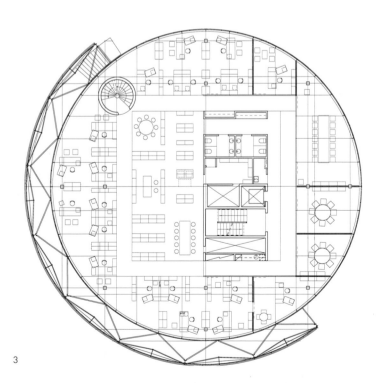

1

3

mcdonald's milan ATELIER MENDINI

THE offices in Milan for McDonald's Italia could be mistaken for a stage set. The designer, Atelier Mendini, has created a vibrant backdrop to work within this creative environment. First impressions blend a mix of corporate branding and 1950s pop art iconography to bombard the visitor with images that create a feeling of dynamism, energy and youth culture.

The 'Ronald McDonald' figure, seated in front of a yellow reception desk, reminds people that this is a consumer products company that owns some of the world's most powerful brand imagery in terms of colour, shape and symbolism. These have been used to effect within the workplace, for example in the main seating area where a bold decorative motif plays on the 'big M' logo.

The office environment seems remote from the initial impact of the entrance, but in fact it is no less dramatic with vibrant colours and an unusual floor plan that creates a central curved spine of cellular spaces that splits the office in two. PVC resin flooring and bold blocks of primary colour help maintain a sense of fun and the unexpected, reflected back by the unusual aluminium ceiling tiles that create a neutral backdrop to the vibrancy of the environment below.

Within the workplace itself, clusters of four workstations are located either side of the sinuous central spine of rooms, where a sense of openness has been maintained by using glazed partitioning with frosted horizontal bands. Classic furniture by Charles Eames together with the more subdued colours in these central areas creates an atmosphere of quiet efficiency that presents a calming environment to contrast with the vibrancy of the other areas.

This office sets out to be original and to break the mould of uniformity that characterizes most fast food architecture. In fact the architect deliberately used references from pop culture and the vocabulary of comics, and in doing so has created a warm and friendly workplace.

location
milan, italy

client
mcdonald's italia company

completed
1997

total floor space
2,000 square metres
(21,530 square feet)

staff
130 people

cost
£460,000

1

2

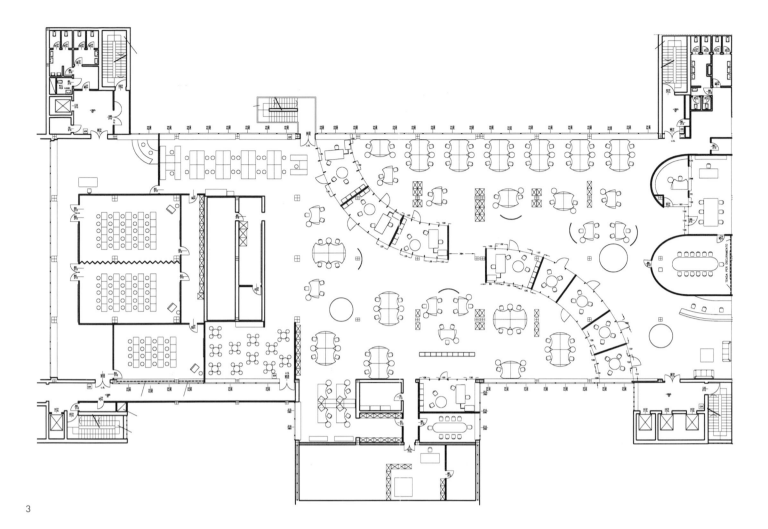

3

4

1 Glazed private
offices with frosted
horizontal bands.

2 Full height glazed
partitions provide a
degree of privacy but
maintain sight lines.

3 Floor plan showing the
central curved spine
of offices that divides
the space.

4 Open-plan workstations
with pop art
as a backdrop.

british airways   **NIELS TORP**

WHEN British Airways briefed architectural practice Niels Torp to design a head-quarters building close to Heathrow Airport that would bring together 2,500 people from 14 locations into one workplace for the first time, the aim was to create a community based on openness and team working – and reflect the airline's new inclusive 'citizen of the world' corporate identity.

The result is a group of six buildings or 'houses', known collectively as Waterside. Each 'house' has a different theme from world geography and sits along a central street 175 metres (570 feet) long. The covered street, a development of Torp's famous 1988 Scandinavian Air Service building in Stockholm, is not just the focus for the whole building but an active work environment towards which people gravitate to collaborate, meet, greet and eat. From the underground car park, staff are directed to emerge into the 'street', which forms a central thoroughfare as well as providing a stimulating atmosphere. Complete with fountains, specially grown trees and Andy Goldsworthy sculpture, the street has been designed to facilitate a change in the way people behave at work.

A library extends into the space, with a sweeping terrace and balcony overlooking an 'olive grove' that provides a place for contemplation. Next to this is the plaza, an area that provides places for people to meet and a speaker's corner where staff can gather in a forum-like environment. The street also features a café, espresso bar, supermarket and florist, and ends at a circular restaurant with views over the gardens, lakes and Japanese bridges.

The building heralds a new era of work practice for British Airways. People work where they need to, not sitting in rigid departments, and use the common areas as a part of their workplace. The concept is to provide 'legible space', grouping teams of six to eight people into defined areas that feel like rooms, but without walls.

Advanced technology is fundamental to Waterside and has been integrated into the building design. Internal cordless telephones allow people to make and receive telephone calls anywhere in the building or the surrounding gardens, while radio links for portable computers allow people to connect from a café table on the central street.

Niels Torp's design has set new standards in workplace architecture for British Airways and at the same time has facilitated innovative thinking about how a headquarters community should function. With Waterside, perhaps British Airways has created the 'world's favourite office building'.

location
london, UK

client
british airways

completed
june 1998

total floor space
3,250 square metres
(35,000 square feet)

staff
2,500 people

cost
£200 million

1

1   The dramatic entrance
    to the new headquarters
    of British Airways.

2   The main street,
    featuring Andy
    Goldsworthy sculpture,
    creates a sense of
    community bringing
    people together
    to interact as well as
    providing areas for
    privacy and
    contemplation.

2

1

1 The office areas are all
  open plan, designed
  to be 'team based and
  team spaced'.

2 View into the Quest
  centre on the main street,
  which acts as a
  knowledge exchange and
  information resource.

2

1, 2 Sections of the building

3 The headquarters consists of six horseshoe-
shaped buildings or 'houses' based around the
central street.

4 Bridges or 'lanes' cross the street and combine
with balconies, staircases and transparent
lifts to create open circulation routes
that encourage people to interact and use
these central shared areas.

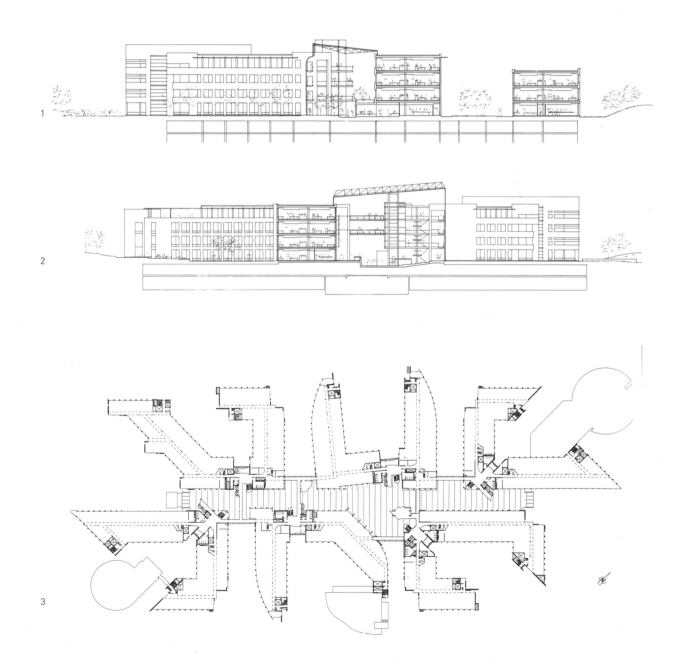

1

2

3

4

LVA   BEHNISCH, BEHNISCH & PARTNER

THE new headquarters of German insurance company LVA has become known collo-
quially as 'the star building'. It is both an innovatively formed office and a shining
example of workplace architecture which responds imaginatively to the complex
requirements of the client's brief. Architects Behnisch, Behnisch & Partner faced not
just the organizational demands of LVA for a modern workplace but also the planning
constraints imposed by the Lubek local authorities to create a building sympathetic to
the massing of the medieval town centre.

As a focal point to the complex, Behnisch designed a dramatic, chaotic entrance
located at the centre of the star, which is also a hub for the workplace. It is here that
staff are encouraged to meet informally and to gather for events and functions. This
space features a series of converging circulation routes that draw people through a
range of facilities, including a restaurant and library.

The architect has been astute in mitigating the giant scale that often destroys any
interaction between people in buildings of this size. Throughout the workplace, smaller 'centres of gravity' (towards which staff are drawn) have been created to allow people to collaborate and dwell in 'sunspots' – key open communication areas designed
to provide a stimulating atmosphere for short, informal meetings. In these sunspots,
tea and coffee points, designed as open kitchens with elegant, café-like surroundings
give views of the landscape outside.

In fact the needs of the individual have been placed above those of the organization, creating a bright, open environment that provides a human scale. The building is
naturally lit and ventilated, and users can control their local environment, adjusting
lighting, heating and sun shading.

The workspaces are located around the perimeter of the buildings, and the narrow floor plate affords all desks a view of the surroundings. The offices are semi-open
plan, with clusters of desks within each room. These private spaces are complemented by a collection of conference rooms, each with a different geometry, that provide a stimulating environment for meetings.

The building helps provide a new sense of community at LVA, bringing people
together for the first time from a number of different locations in the town. Through
the integration of work and leisure, a new
home for the business and a modern landmark for Lubek has been created.

location
lubek, germany

client
landesversicherungsanstalt
schleswig-holstein

completed
may 1997

total floor space
37,110 square metres
(399,450 square feet)

staff
1,000 people

cost
DM156 million

1   Site plan showing the
    star-shaped building.

2   The chaotic central
    focal point with its
    converging stairways and
    circulation routes that
    pull people together.

1

1 Main restaurant and
   central meeting
   place for staff where
   hanging fluorescent
   light fittings and
   the bold use of colour
   have created a lively
   and dynamic setting.

2 The building provides
   a variety of places
   for people to work, both
   inside and outside
   including the gardens
   and landscaped roof
   top areas.

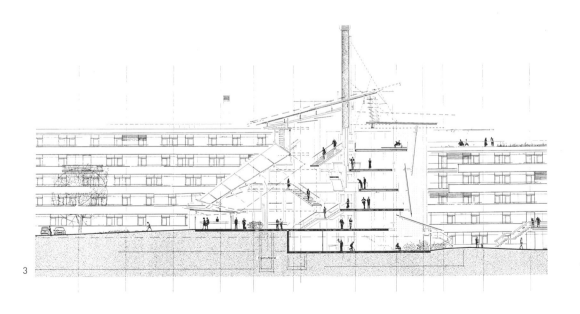

2

3 Section

2

5

3

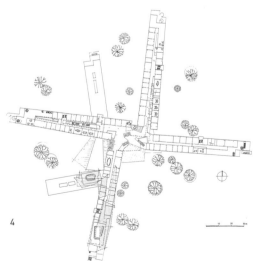

4

1 Converging and crossing
circulation routes and
staircases bring people
together, creating the
opportunity for chance
encounters or informal
meetings, and fostering
the sense of community.

2 Ground floor plan

3 Third floor plan

4 Fourth floor plan

5 One of the 'sun spots'
located at key points
around the building
where staff are
encouraged to dwell and
chat over coffee.

1

office-daiwa TORU MURAKAMI

THIS minimalist space creates a contemplative atmosphere within a workplace based on the principles of Zen. Spaces that are described by clean surfaces and light, transparent materials form a series of meeting rooms and offices for Daiwa, a Japanese fountain maintenance company. As a company for which water is a central part of the product, it is not surprising that this office makes use of lakes and pools to create a reflective, almost serene mood. The tranquil spaces provide a neutral backdrop for the corporate activities that occur within them, and have been designed to project a calming atmosphere.

Within this peaceful environment lies a well-conceived plan that creates a series of workplaces within the L-shaped building. A single-storey complex of meeting spaces and a two-storey accommodation block provide an office that is based around a central, enclosed courtyard. Furniture and storage within the complex are finished in white, as are the floor and ceiling. Together they create a clean feel that combines with the full height glazed panels to provide a light, translucent and uncluttered environment.

This building creates a thoughtful workplace, using water to project a feeling of quiet efficiency and professionalism and to reflect the company's core business. At the same time it does not make an overtly corporate statement, reinforcing its local ties through a transparency that ensures the building is seen to be an extension of the local environment and a part of the community.

location
tsuyama, japan

client
daiwa

completed
june 1995

total floor space
455 square metres
(4,900 square feet)

staff
30 people

cost
undisclosed

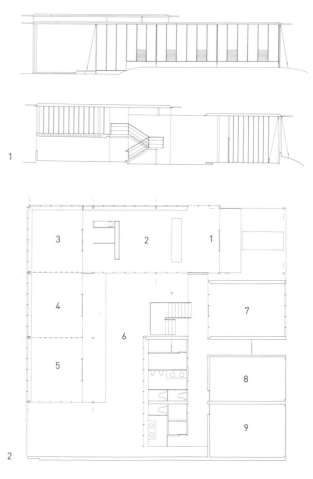

1

2

1 Section and north elevation

2 First floor plan
 Key
 1 Entrance
 2 Office
 3 Executive's room
 4 Reception room
 5 President's room
 6 Courtyard
 7 Hydraulic laboratory
 8 Storage
 9 Parking

3 Zen minimalism with reflective water and transparent office environments that integrate the workplace with its surroundings.

3

bürohaus   KAUFFMANN THEILIG & PARTNER

THE rotunda that forms the headquarters of this German software company provides both a striking landmark building and a workplace that breaks with tradition. Following the contours of its hill site, the circular shape of the building is meant to be symbolic as it points in no particular direction; the 'doughnut' plan has been designed to break down hierarchy and barriers by creating a sense of workplace community.

Architects Kauffmann Theilig & Partner designed the arc-like structure to create a large central space that is spanned by a striking glazed roof structure. This atrium provides a focus for the building where all viewpoints and pathways meet. A large proportion of the office has been given to this space, which, according to the architects, forms the 'functional and emotional heart of the building'. A dramatic open staircase hanging in the atrium connects the floors and provides a vertical link for the building – from ground floor café to upper galleries. Additionally a series of bridges serve to bring people together.

All the workspaces span off the central atrium and have been designed to encourage collaboration and team work. Clusters of desks in either open or cellular space have been designed for flexibility, allowing groups to change continuously. Most of the partitions are glazed, providing a feel of openness and translucency that gives employees a sense of working together. The private spaces afford access to public areas on both the inside and outside of the building, where a balcony extends from the façade to provide both an informal social space for meetings and a sunscreen to prevent glare in the offices below.

The untreated materials used in construction, mainly concrete and wood, give the building a raw and natural feel. This was intentional, as the bare surfaces store energy and allow the building to be conditioned naturally: heat generated by people and equipment warms the office in winter and air that has been through an underground duct cools the facility in summer.

With its dominant atrium space and non-linear form, the chief attributes of a mould-breaking design, this is a project that enhances the opportunities for people to work together in a more communal way.

1

location
gniebel, germany

client
data-firmengruppe

completed
1996

total floor space
5,672 square metres
(61,030 square feet)

staff
250 people

cost
DM 14.5 million

1   The symbolic circular building with its external balconies and dramatic glazed roof.

2   Main atrium space provides a focus for the community and a place for people to meet informally.

1 Balconies allow people to step outside for fresh air and provide places for chance encounters.

2 Floor plan showing the private and public spaces.

3 Section

4 One of the upper galleries that encourages circulation around the building.

1

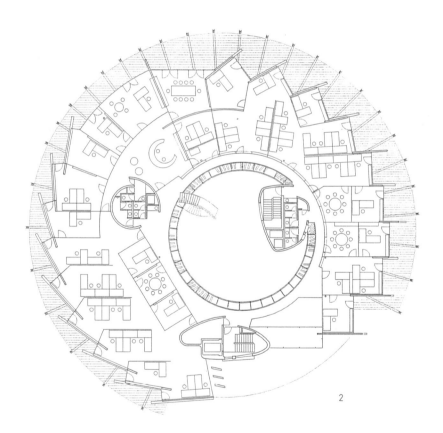

2

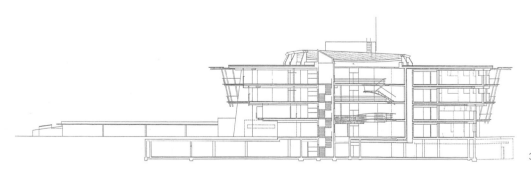

3

4

yapi kredi bank   JOHN McASLAN & PARTNERS

ON a site overlooking the Sea of Marmara, architect John McAslan & Partners has created an operations and data centre in a new building that is one of the largest of its kind in Europe. Designed for Yapi Kredi, Turkey's largest private bank, the office complex has been modelled on traditional Middle Eastern urban structures to create a community for the 1,800 workers who are based there.

A glazed bridge that spans a landscaped ravine creates a dramatic arrival for visitors to the centre; it leads to a plaza that provides a canopied main entrance into the complex of buildings and spaces forming what is, in effect, an office city.

The master plan breaks up the site into ten three-storey buildings, partly to create a human scale and partly as a precaution against earthquakes, as each block is structurally independent. These buildings are connected by a series of covered internal streets that form the heart of the community, recreating the atmosphere of the bazaar both in terms of intended use and through the design. A flexible fabric roof structure spans the street together with strips of glass and retractable blinds that allow a managed degree of daylight to enter the space.

The architect has based the concept for these common areas on the model of the *Han*, the places where merchants stopped on their journeys to rest and trade. Offices are grouped around central courts that provide shared spaces, and at each street junction a distinctive cylindrical structure forms a common landmark; this is a striking architectural feature providing access to the workspaces as well as services for the buildings.

Each street has been designed differently, with interior planting throughout the complex to distinguish spaces. The design encourages interaction between people in different departments in the centre, providing places to work away from the traditional desk or meeting room.

Within the office environment, the mostly open-plan space creates an ordered atmosphere to contrast with the bustle of the streets outside. Modern Dutch-made Ahrend office furniture has been used, with desks clustered in groups of four. Sight lines have been maintained through the use of low screens and storage elements. Overall the building has achieved the desired need to encourage both collaboration and concentrated work, creating a community within a space designed to bring people together.

1   Section showing the building and entrance bridge.

2   One of the streets complete with trees and a café as well as the cylindrical staircase that leads to the office floors.

location
gebze, turkey

client
yapi kredi bank operations centre

completed
1997

total floor space
50,000 square metres
(538,210 square feet)

staff
1,800 people

cost
£20 million

2

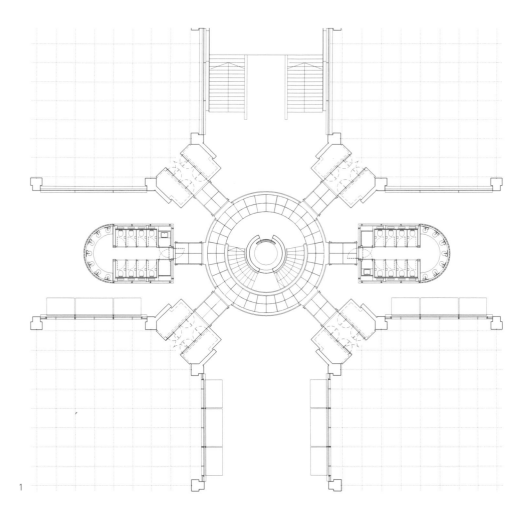

1

1 Plan of the crossroads
between two streets showing
central services cylinder.

2 Site plan illustrating
the office 'city' with ten
separate buildings
and the adjoining streets.

3 Canopied main entrance
with its dramatic glazed
suspension bridge
that crosses a ravine.

3

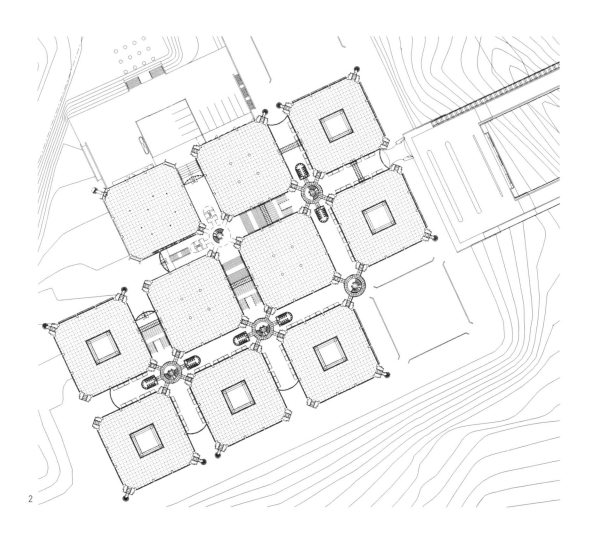

2

1 The garden square
and sculptural spiral
staircases that
encourage people to
move between floors.

2 The streets have been
modelled on the
Han as places where
merchants stopped
on their journeys
to rest and trade.

2

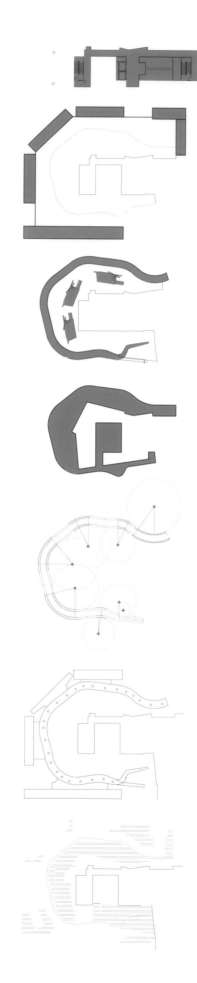

shr perceptual management

MORPHOSIS

THIS 'community office' concept was developed by Morphosis for the US offices of design firm SHR. The workplace has been cleverly divided into different zones that distinguish activities within the space. The U-shaped building footprint has been used to good effect, creating an office community that locates cellular space around the perimeter of the floor, using a continuous wall of office partitions that bends and folds its way in an arc from one end of the space to the other.

The inner, enclosed space provides for a flexible conference and meeting area as well as open-plan workstations. Each of the three areas inside the white 'tube' of workstations is an 'oasis', providing a work setting that gives a contrasting atmosphere to the enclosed areas. The screens of perforated metal that float above these collaborative areas demarcate these zones.

Shown here are typical floor plans and computer realizations of the scheme, illustrating the narrative quality of the interior.

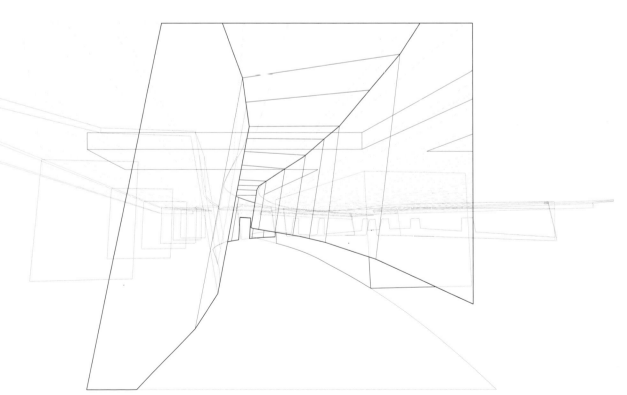

mobilit

Y OFFICES were once static and sedentary places to work. People sat at fixed locations under the constant gaze of a supervisor. Both management control and technological constraint anchored the office worker to the spot. But in the creative office, movement from place to place is encouraged as people work how and where they want within the building or campus, supported by new and cordless technologies. The concept of mobility allows work to become a series of journeys which create chance encounters and informal meetings that are all the more productive because they are spontaneous and unplanned. This final section shows a range of office interiors which support mobile work patterns.

monsanto   HOLEY ASSOCIATES

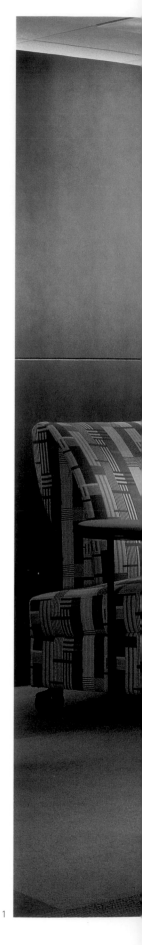

SUCH terms as 'meadow', 'porch', 'parlour' and 'seasonal spaces' describe a workplace that represents not just the leading-edge business of life sciences company Monsanto, but also the innovative thinking and design development that lies behind its headquarters facility. This is a scheme that encourages users to rethink their preconceptions of an office as they embrace new ways of working and alternative places in which to work.

Monsanto realized that it could gain competitive advantage by creating a working environment that enabled its people to outperform the competition. This pilot phase of a much larger 37,160 square metre (400,000 square foot) project involved creating future workplace concepts for the company's senior executives. A mix of public and private areas as well as static and dynamic spaces sets the scene for people who are free to choose their work setting as they move from the public 'meadow' into one of a series of neighbourhoods that define an environment.

Each neighbourhood provides a sense of community for a group or business team; a place where people can choose a setting from a range of environments that include the study with its shared resources, the parlour for private meetings or telephone calls, and the den, which is personal workspace.

In moving from public to private, an intermediary area has been developed that is known as the porch. This semi-private area can be adapted by the individual to recreate the behaviour of people sitting on porches: facing outwards when receptive to unexpected conversations with passers-by or turned away to signal that privacy is desired.

The space planning encourages informal and ad hoc interaction as people move between different areas of the floor. With its unexpected circulation, the individual's journey is directed through a range of semi-private spaces. In recreating familiar signposts, the architects, Holey Associates, contributed to the success of the project by giving people a sense of ownership of the space. This sentiment extends to the technology used in the building where, for example, cordless infra-red controllers allow users to change their local environment by altering the lighting and heating in their immediate vicinity.

In fact Holey Associates has created an integrated approach to mobile work through the analogy with rural ranch settings, demonstrating that better working practices can be achieved by thinking of an environment as a total workplace as opposed to a collection of individual workspaces.

location
st louis, missouri, usa

client
monsanto company

completed
november 1997

total floor space
3,250 square metres
(35,000 square feet)

staff
75 people

cost
undisclosed

1 The 'front porch' affords
   a degree of privacy but at
   the same time provides
   a place for people to have
   informal conversations
   as they pass through
   the space.

1 The 'meadow', complete with
circulation areas, café
and 'seasonal spaces',
provides a place for dynamic
interaction in a shared or
public environment that
can be reconfigured easily for
different functions.

2 Floor plan showing the
allocation of space that
provides variety within each
neighbourhood. The user
moves from the meadow into
one of the team areas or
neighbourhoods shown in
yellow and illustrated in detail
by the furniture layout below.

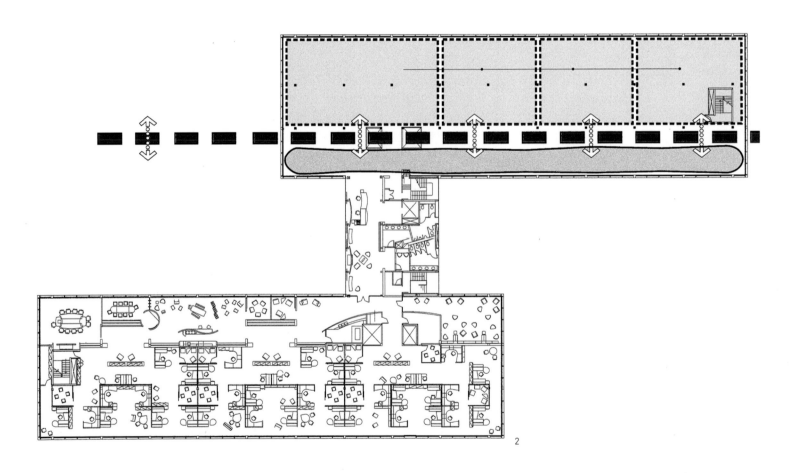

1

2

1 The square is a central area that becomes the focus of the community on each floor. All circulation routes converge here, providing a place for chance encounters and a reception area where visitors are greeted.

2 A library area that gives people a thoughtful space, providing a quiet alternative to the public interaction spaces. There are intentionally no telephones here and the casual furniture creates a contrasting atmosphere to the office areas.

3 View into a neighbourhood, showing individual workstations or 'dens' together with a room or 'parlour' for private meetings or conversations.

arthur andersen **BDG McCOLL**

THE business consulting division of international accountancy firm Arthur Andersen has created an innovative and team-based workspace within its London headquarters. Based on the ethos of flexible working, it allows a group of 170 people access to advanced resources and a choice of working environment.

Within the space itself, dramatic colours have been used to good effect, influenced by the lateral thinking of guru Edward de Bono. Design consultants BDG McColl have created red meeting rooms to energize and green rooms to stimulate creativity. They have also cleverly combined commercial and domestic furniture to produce an atmosphere that mixes formal with informal and creates dramatic contrasts as the individual moves through the space.

The client's objective was to establish an environment in which personal business relationships could be built and learning between teams could take place. With an emphasis on so-called 'brain aerobics' and the physical well-being of Arthur Andersen's staff, a place for the changing needs of a transient workforce was the brief that had to be answered.

As its focus, the designers have created a hub behind the reception area where guests are greeted. This hub has been planned as a café with simple metal tables and chairs that create a relaxed atmosphere where people can meet informally. The central area also divides the long space into two distinctive parts, one for concentrated work and the other for collaborative work.

Within the 'Zen' environment for quiet work, fish tanks and visuals of palm trees create a calming atmosphere, while at the opposite end of the spectrum, the team-work area has been dubbed 'chaos'. Here people reconfigure the mobile furniture to suit the task at hand and create team spaces as needed. The mobility and flexibility of the consultants' environment is contrasted by the team administrators who all have permanent desks, providing a focus for project information that is stored nearby.

The use of curves in both the storage wall for lockers and the bench for hot-desking positions produces a fluid effect that creates a feeling of movement throughout the workplace. With this sense of motion and the need to move between noisy, interactive and quiet areas during the working day, a dynamic space has been created that encourages collaboration and interaction, responding to the way Arthur Andersen consultants think as well as their various workplace tasks.

location
london, UK

client
arthur andersen

completed
november 1997

total floor space
820 square metres
(8,800 square feet)

staff
170 people

cost
undisclosed

1

1 View into the main shared office area showing the non-reservable desks and the raised bench where people can work on laptop computers for a temporary period of time. A curved wall and dropped ceiling identify the circulation route and provide an element of demarcation.

2 Floor plan showing the subdivision of the narrow space into defined zones.

1 Coloured meeting rooms based on de Bono's theories of the 'coloured hats', where red is designed to energize and blue to calm.

2 The Internet zone, where people can perch on stools and access the Internet through state-of-the-art flat screens and network computers.

3 Centralized storage provides shared information that is focused around support staff who are assigned permanent workstations.

4 The 'chaos zone' features Fantoni mobile tables and Herman Miller's Aeron chair. Behind is a curved storage wall with purpose-built lockers to give people a degree of personalized storage, complete with a central cupboard and two smaller units for a laptop computer and 'in-tray'.

ideo san francisco

IDEO & BAUM THORNLEY ARCHITECTS

WHEN IDEO, the international product development company, decided to move to a new office in San Francisco, an old waterfront warehouse fulfilled the brief for a dynamic and adaptable space. With its character, openness and broad sight lines, together with spectacular views across the bay, the building allowed the creation of a workspace that reflected the philosophy and culture of IDEO San Francisco and embraced the consulting firm's concept of mobile working.

Mobility is central to IDEO's work philosophy – both inside and outside the office. Being mobile at work started with the premise of not having an assigned desk or office but instead a range of places in which to work in different areas of the building. It was then extended to enable staff to work outside this workplace.

IDEO realized that technology had changed the rules. Equipped with portable Powerbooks and cordless telephones, IDEO's mobile workers can choose their work setting – from a library or team room inside the office to a car or café outside in the urban environment.

Baum Thornley Architects, working alongside IDEO designers, created an unusual environment to reflect and encourage this fluid and varying working style. With its 'Wing' to house the studio and its 'Wall' to provide defined client areas, the architect has divided the space into private and public areas.

Within the workplace, collaboration has been encouraged by creating a series of eleven islands or clusters that give teams of four people their own legible area. This is central to IDEO's culture of integrating people from different design, engineering and computing disciplines into a project team. The islands, designed by Sam Hecht and Ian Coats MacColl, are connected together along a central spine and a system of mobile tables has been developed to allow users to reconfigure their environment for the task at hand.

Within the public areas, semi-enclosed team rooms allow for formal meetings while areas such as the café and the lookout provide more casual settings for interaction, collaboration and informal meetings. Based on the principles of communication, adaptability and mobility, IDEO has created an effective workspace that serves the changing needs of its people and provides a stimulating and creative environment in which they can develop innovative new products.

1

location
san francisco, USA

client
IDEO

completed
january 1996

total floor space
1,115 square metres
(12,000 square feet)

staff
40 people

cost
£0.5 million

1 Baum Thornley Architects have designed a dynamic space for IDEO's studio in San Francisco, combining wood and glass to create a light, open environment.

2 The old warehouse space provides a flexible environment that can be used for presentations and events as well as informal meetings. A dramatic glazed screen can be lowered to subdivide the space.

1   Leading off the main
    circulation route are
    sliding doors that provide
    semi-enclosed team
    rooms. The curved wing of
    translucent fibreglass is an
    extension of the canopied
    ceiling over the rooms.

2   Floor plan illustrating the
    curved spines of desking
    and the separation of private
    and public spaces.

3   Furniture axonometric
    illustrating one of
    the islands that populate
    the space, providing
    a central bookcase and
    team table as well
    as four workstations.

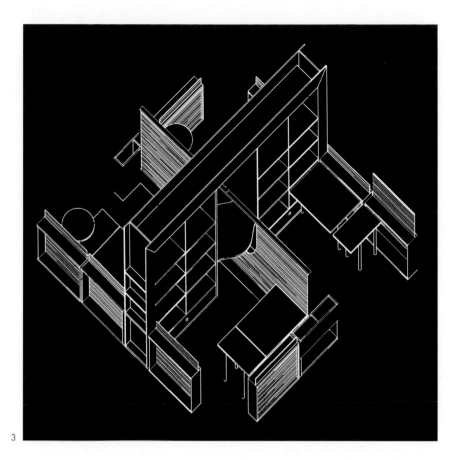

1

2

1 The main reception area allows
   visitors a clear view across
   the office. The old industrial
   space has been retained in
   character, and clear sight lines
   have been achieved to encourage
   collaboration.

2 At the end of the studio is the
   lookout, a café and meeting space
   that leads on to a balcony
   with spectacular views across
   San Francisco bay.

3 Axonometric of the workplace,
   illustrating the juxtaposition
   of different work settings for
   individual endeavour and
   group interaction. The fluid and
   varying work styles of IDEO's staff
   have been taken into account
   and the design of the studio
   encourages cross-disciplinary
   communication.

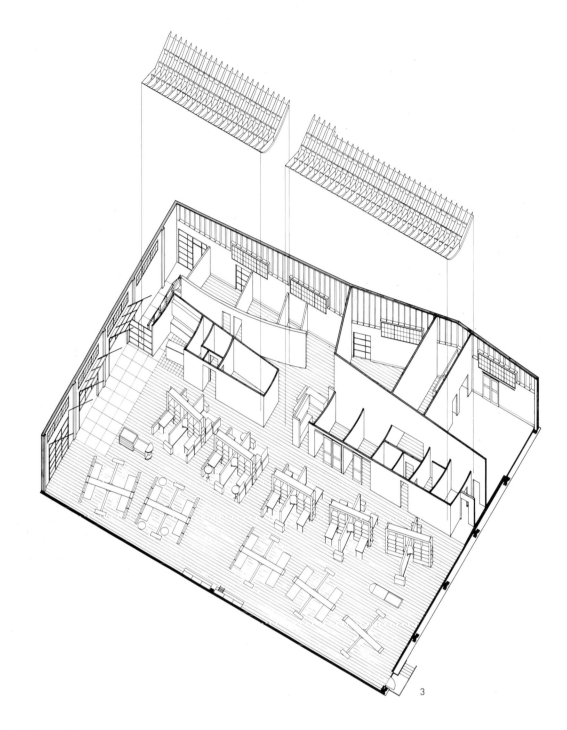

3

1

2

ideo tokyo   SAM HECHT

THIS small-scale but innovative solution for IDEO's drop-in Tokyo office shows that flexible work environments are applicable even for a handful of people. The thinking behind the design is to give visiting associates a temporary home in Japan that provides for both individual effort and teamwork. In its essence it is a very furniture-led solution using a combination of materials and finishes to create a functional space.

IDEO designer Sam Hecht has combined his knowledge of workplace futures with furniture design to create a collection of unusual pieces that allow for flexibility and mobility within the space. Each person can use a number of furniture elements – from a translucent mobile hoteling trolley that allows others to see what is being carried, to a wall cabinet with doors that may be opened to provide a degree of privacy.

The two-part workstation has a cherry desk and curved Formica table that combine to create a flexible and adaptable worktool. Limited cable management and an Italian task light (by Artemide) complete the work setting. To aid familiarity and effectiveness, people arriving at IDEO's compact Tokyo office are provided with a comfort kit that contains everything from a name tag and Post-it notes to a packet of sweets.

It is IDEO's working philosophy that each office within its global network has a degree of autonomy which allows it to create its own working culture. Thus IDEO's Japanese office – a simple, highly edited, yet elegant solution where mobile workers can spend time productively despite the lack of space – is very different from IDEO San Francisco where a more spacious waterfront building has led to a different interpretation of new work styles.

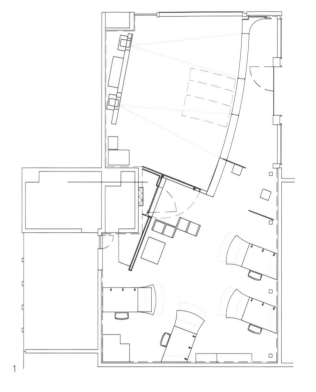

1

location
tokyo, japan

client
IDEO

completed
november 1994

total floor space
70 square metres
(750 square feet)

staff
5 people

cost
£60,000

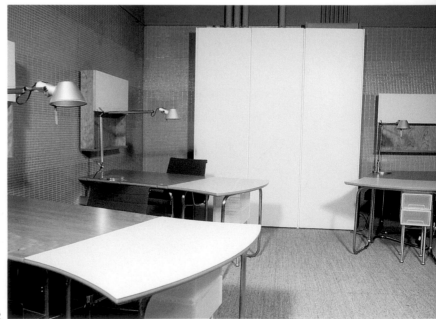

2

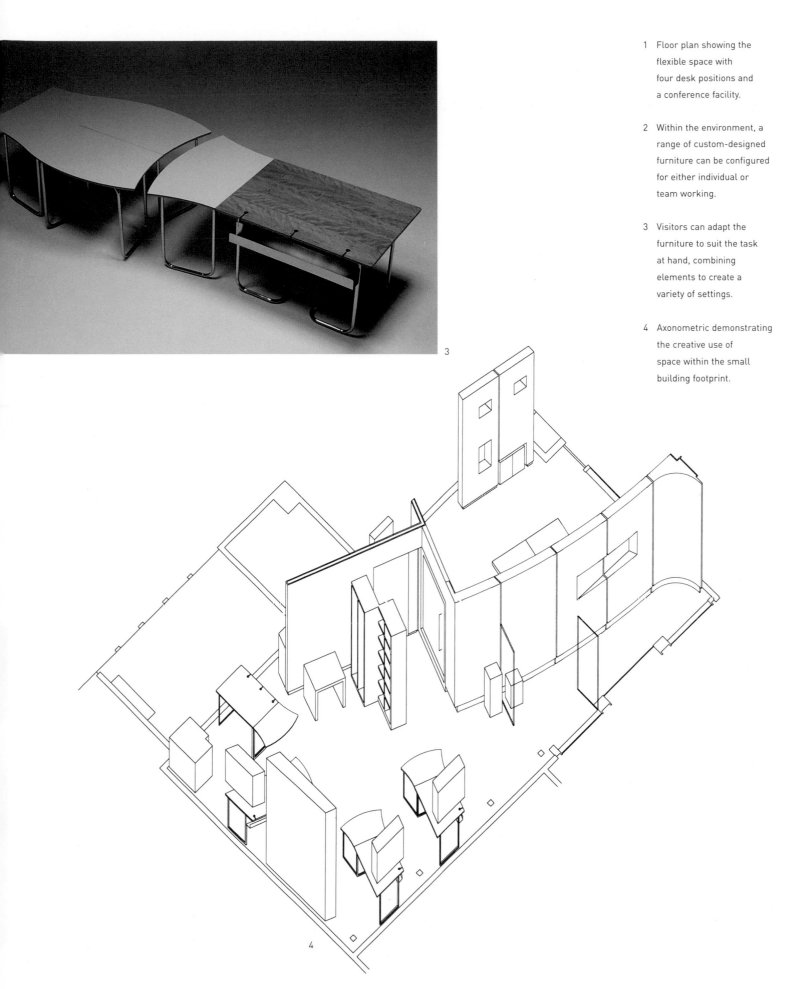

1   Floor plan showing the
    flexible space with
    four desk positions and
    a conference facility.

2   Within the environment, a
    range of custom-designed
    furniture can be configured
    for either individual or
    team working.

3   Visitors can adapt the
    furniture to suit the task
    at hand, combining
    elements to create a
    variety of settings.

4   Axonometric demonstrating
    the creative use of
    space within the small
    building footprint.

3

4

m&c saatchi   HARPER MACKAY

FOR advertising agency M&C Saatchi the move to its first London home after the high-profile split from the original Saatchi & Saatchi agency was important and the building itself was designed to express its aspirations for success through rapid growth. Carved out of two adjacent properties in London's Golden Square, the scheme by architect Harper Mackay has physically linked the buildings together, creating a large atrium space that dominates the headquarters and provides the workplace with a central focus.

The design concept uses this square outside as a virtual reception area or vestibule, relegating the reception area to an entrance hall. This was achieved by introducing a new front door at the centre of the main façade, thereby creating symmetry and an axis from the square through to the centre of the building.

Perhaps the most interesting feature of the atrium is its inside/outside design. This ambiguous existence describes its dual role as an internal courtyard extending off the main reception, and an external façade for the office floors and work areas where glazed balconies imply an aspect on to other disparate spaces.

The creation of the new front door not only gives an imposing sense of arrival but allows the ground floor to become a central crossroads. Its importance is emphasized by the slightly exaggerated or oversized reception desk, espresso bar and seating areas that give an 'Alice in Wonderland' effect. The central space encourages people to dwell and meet informally and creates a buzz at the heart of this creative workplace.

Moving away from the ground floor, the central staircase has been engineered to take people away from the symmetry and create an experience that the designers describe as rotational, developing surprise on the journey as people move from common areas to work environments.

Here again there has been an intentional policy to present the unexpected. In contrast to traditional advertising environments, creatives working in teams of two occupy carousels, as opposed to cellular offices. These semi-enclosed spaces allow a high degree of visibility and have no doors to encourage collaboration, yet they are also designed to provide privacy.

At the top of the building, the four partners also occupy a collaborative space, where desks have been replaced by clear glass workbenches that span the length of the building. Together with a central informal area, this dramatic space provides a flexible and adaptable environment that encourages teamwork and creates a calming and stimulating workplace.

location
london, UK

client
m & c saatchi

completed
november 1997

total floor space
5,575 square metres
(60,000 square feet)

staff
200 people

cost
£4.5 million

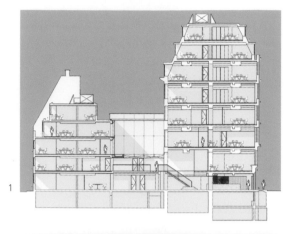

1

2

1   Section showing the two adjacent buildings that have been linked by a central atrium.

2   The new main entrance into the buildings from Golden Square illustrating the symmetry of the space and the dramatic sense of arrival.

3   View across the atrium showing the café on the ground floor and the work areas. A bold three-dimensional logo dominates the upper floors.

3

1

1 Encouraging mobility within the
   workplace, this impressive
   staircase provides a dramatic
   feature and creates a crossroads,
   bringing people together into the
   central courtyard that provides
   shared informal meeting spaces
   and facilities.

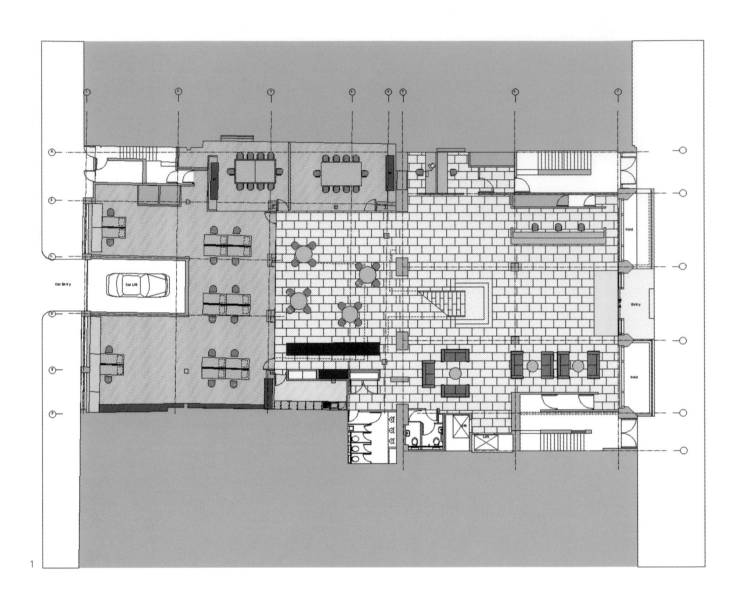

1   Car Entry   Car Lift   Entry

1   Ground floor plan demonstrating
the clear sight lines from front to
back and the slightly oversized
reception desk and café bar that
dominate the space.

2   The open-plan work areas have been
designed to improve communication
and facilitate creativity.

3   Collaborative space designed for
the four partners provides a
light, open environment that uses
glazed walls and desking to
create a stimulating workplace.

2

3

f/x networks   FERNAU & HARTMAN

FOX Tower in downtown Los Angeles is the location for an unusual headquarters office. Cable company f/X Networks occupies one floor of the skyscraper building in a scheme that has been designed to be non-hierarchical, inverting the traditional assumptions of typical high-rise office space. Cellular offices occupy the inner core and the perimeter space has been given to circulation, common and team areas. Executives sit in one of 37 small cubicles while support and administrative staff sit at desks in the bright and open space that extends to windows that overlook the Pacific Ocean and the city.

These views have been used to good effect, as the local work setting has been themed to reflect the associated external environment. The ramps to the conference rooms look out over hills, while in the 'lot', programming staff are afforded a view of the real Twentieth Century Fox movie lot where the programmes are made.

In the office, everyone starts their day by visiting the 'lifeguard station', a room opposite the senior vice president's cubicle, where they pick up mail, get refreshments or 'check conditions' before either moving to their workspace or 'hitting the beach', an area that provides fold-out desks for temporary staff.

In this workplace, 'empty' space is viewed as valuable space. It is here that the real work of the company takes place, either in one of seven eccentric areas that serve as conference rooms or in the spaces in between the grid of permanent cubicles and desks that have been supplemented with mobile furniture pieces for ad hoc meetings. Here, deck chairs around picnic tables with rolling blackboards provide flexible space for a mobile workforce.

As with another keynote broadcast office scheme for Nickelodeon in New York, architects Fernau & Hartman have used colour and materials to good effect to add to the unusual planning and thinking that underpins the workplace. From the use of an exposed assembly that looks like scaffolding to a creative 'sweat box' that has a sauna-like appearance, they have provided surprise and the unexpected in a workplace that breaks the rules.

This even extends to the way they have peeled the building back to the core, exposing services and creating the spaces that enable the design solution to work. This office challenges the user and reinforces the spirit of a company based upon openness and teamwork.

location
los angeles, USA

client
f/x networks, fox inc.

completed
november 1995

total floor space
2,785 square metres
(30,000 square feet)

staff
102 people

cost
undisclosed

1

1 Fox Tower provides a dramatic setting for this unusual workspace.

2 The lifeguard station, which resembles a beach shack, provides a central place where people meet each morning. Much of the floor space is given over to circulation, encouraging mobility and allowing people to hold informal meetings in unusual settings such as the deck chairs with their view over the Pacific Ocean.

2

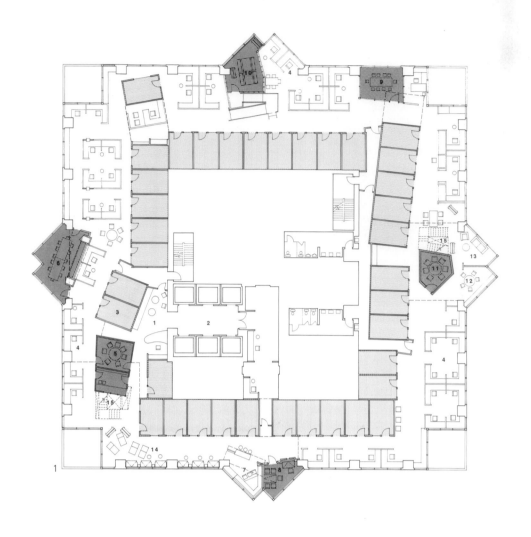

1

2

3

1   Floor plan illustrating:

1 Reception area
2 Lobby
3 Typical closed office
4 'Murphy' workstations
5 'Lifeguard' conference room
6 Executive conference room
7 'Diner' conference room
8 'Murphy' conference area

9 'Storefront' conference area
10 'The hill' conference area
11 'Sweat box' conference area
12 Conference area
13 Research areas
14 'Beach' conference areas
15 Stairway to 5th floor

2   The 'sweat box' has been
    designed to evoke a sauna
    and provide a place
    for brainstorming and
    creative meetings.

3   The 'hill', a room that is
    almost a non-room, has an
    open skeletal wall structure
    that was inspired by Rudolf
    Schindler's hillside houses.

4   The main reception area
    complete with shark
    fin desk, seating area and
    mobile furniture.

g o d m a n CD PARTNERSHIP

REFLECTING the transient work patterns of its staff, the concept design for the Soho workplace of Godman, an advertising and production company, uses such terms as 'first class lounge' and 'check-in desk' as well as 'arrivals and departures'. With a mobile workforce that includes producers who spend much of their time travelling, the airport analogy seems apt. What has been created by designers CD Partnership is a flexible space that suits both the building and Godman's dynamic business.

Inside a pre-Second World War building that might have lent itself to a standard developer's specification, the interior scheme creates a very raw and simple feel to the loft-type space, avoiding the obvious make-over in favour of natural or existing materials, with basic finishes and exposed services. This allows the environment to be changed and adapted without infrastructure costs. Instead the budget has been focused on key selected and memorable areas.

Against a neutral backdrop, the choice of furniture gives a dramatic splash of colour and adds a feeling of domesticity to the workplace. A number of different types of workspace have been created within the environment, from private offices for the creatives to open-plan workstations for the production staff.

A central theme was to encourage interaction between these two discrete disciplines; the space planning effectively forces people to move through the office to interact with colleagues. This is encouraged by the central positioning of a restaurant-style bar – a semicircular bench with seating that provides a social as well as functional space.

For Godman, first impressions of visitors are important and the designers created an interesting tunnel using industrial glass planks on both ceiling and walls to give a futuristic impact as people move through this space to the lounge or work areas. Apart from the chosen focal points, the thinking is very much about stripping the scheme to its bare skin, with all but essential specification ruled out. This gives the environment its elegant simplicity. The project demonstrates the creation of an effective office in which both desk-based and team-based space can co-exist to create a balance between individual and group work.

location
london, UK

client
godman

completed
october 1997

total floor space
695 square metres
(7,500 square feet)

staff
15 people

cost
undisclosed

1 The workplace
encourages collaboration
and provides a
combination of social and
functional spaces that
allow people to use
the space effectively.

2 A dramatic entrance
corridor makes use of
industrial materials,
including glass planks
that provide interest
as people move through
the space.

2

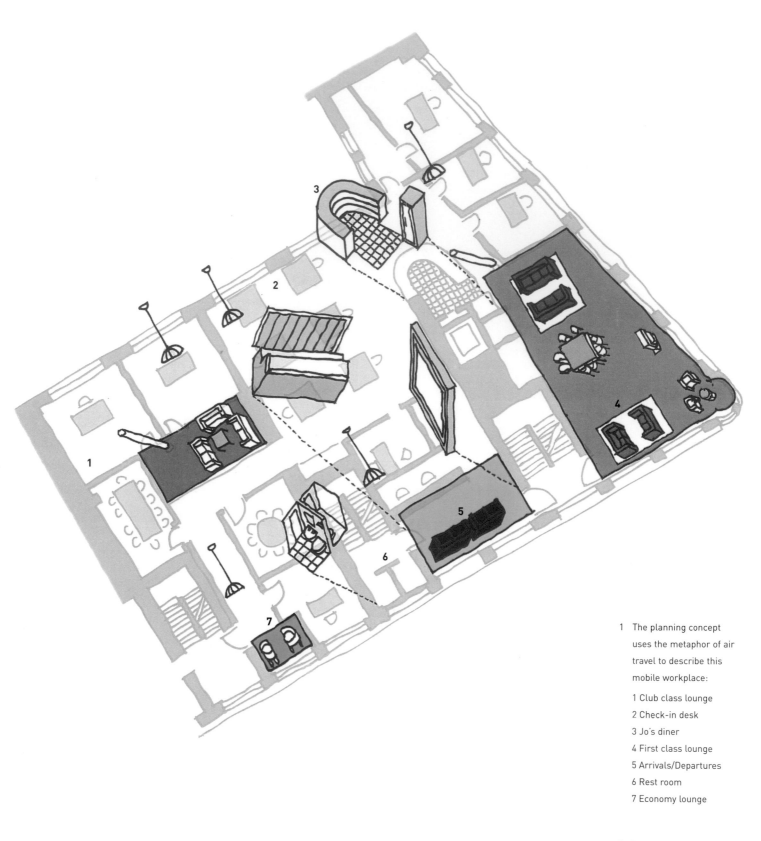

1 The planning concept
uses the metaphor of air
travel to describe this
mobile workplace:

1 Club class lounge
2 Check-in desk
3 Jo's diner
4 First class lounge
5 Arrivals/Departures
6 Rest room
7 Economy lounge

2 Food and drink become
an important part of the
creative office, here
placed centrally through
the design of a
restaurant-style bar that
dominates the space.

owens corning
CESAR PELLI & ASSOCIATES

THE corporate identity of building materials giant Owens Corning is reflected in its world headquarters by Cesar Pelli's 'fish fin' tower. The architect has combined an arc-shaped, three-storey office building with separate elements such as a 'Panther' meeting and auditorium facility, a Discovery training complex and a Wellbeing Centre (including a gym) to create a campus environment in Ohio.

These ancillary buildings are all clad in brick using bright, vibrant colours to contrast with the pure, white, transparent office complex and to emphasize the concept of a collection of different spaces. All the components of this workplace are based around a central courtyard, designed to allow a wide range of use from open-air concerts to dining and informal meetings.

The design of the facility reflects the company's shift from a hierarchical organization, described by its old 28-storey building, to a flatter, horizontal structure that is decentralized, team orientated and dedicated to a global, mobile philosophy. Office areas are open plan and there has been a conscious decision to provide staircases as opposed to lifts, encouraging people to circulate and meet informally.

Owens Corning has combined advanced technology with recent theories on workplace psychology in a building designed to set new standards. Behind its move towards greater mobility and flexibility is the belief that creativity and problem-solving blossom in chance meetings and quiet moments of reflection, as opposed to formal work behind a desk or conference table.

The technology in the building is complex, with more than 2,400 data sockets designed to allow a laptop computer to be used anywhere in the complex. This combines with a Companion cordless office telephone system to allow people to choose their work setting and still be connected.

Pelli's red-brick fin tower provides a focal point for the headquarters and creates a dramatic reception area. Its hollow 20 metre (66 foot) interior rises above the space where a Pelli-designed carpet and curved reception desk sit in the voluminous entrance.

A dramatic vista down the main corridor leads visitors on an interesting journey past the shared facilities to the work areas. This is where the real mould-breaking has taken place, providing workers with both a home base and communal areas that are collaborative and creative.

location
toledo, ohio, USA

client
owens corning

completed
january 1996

total floor space
37,160 square metres
(400,000 square feet)

staff
1,200 people

cost
$116 million

1

1 The campus complex next to the Maumee River in Toledo provides a dramatic setting for the collection of buildings that form the headquarters complex. Clearly visible is the famous red 'fish fin' tower that has become a local landmark.

2 Main reception area underneath the 'fin' with a dramatic curved glass reception desk and carpet designed by Cesar Pelli.

2

1 A three-storey glazed atrium
   space maximizes access to
   daylight and provides external
   views as well as a focal point
   that encourages informal
   interaction or 'casual collisions'
   between people as they
   move around the building.

1

1   The courtyard provides, weather
    permitting, an extension to the
    workplace and is used for
    informal meetings, rest and
    entertainment.

2   Ground floor site plan showing
    the clustering of buildings
    around a central courtyard.

3   First floor plan detail showing
    the restaurant, training facilities
    and a part of the auditorium
    in the bottom left-hand corner.

4   Detail of the space planning on
    a typical office floor illustrating
    the clustering of desks in
    open plan to create team spaces
    with shared meeting tables.

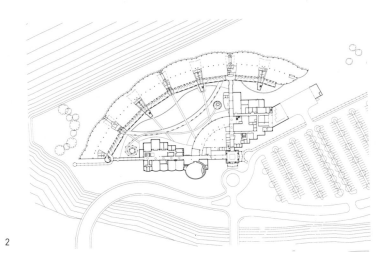

2

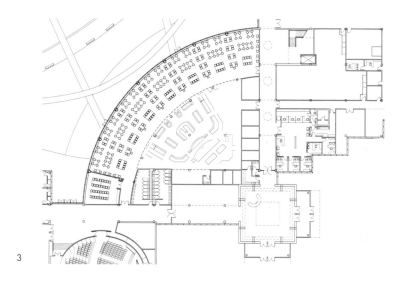

3

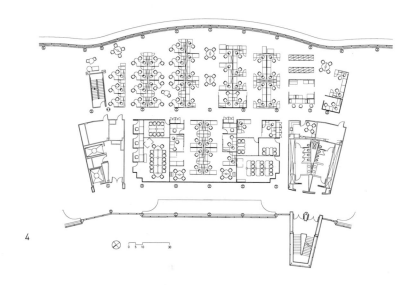

4

DEGW   **DEGW IN-HOUSE TEAM**

FOR workplace architects DEGW, the need to practice what they preach was one of the driving forces behind this completely refurbished workplace. As visionaries on the future of the office, their own space in a former bottling warehouse in King's Cross, London was an ideal place in which to try out new ideas and put their concepts into action.

The result is a stimulating environment for DEGW's staff, some of whom are mobile, some semi-mobile and some sedentary; and a fitting building for the headquarters of a design practice described by chairman Francis Duffy as fascinated by the impact of time and the consequences of change.

The firm's base at Porters North had been converted by DEGW into design offices in the late 1980s – an innovative conversion at the time, with exposed services and raw materials. In less than a decade, however, workplace concepts had moved on and new life needed to be breathed into the project. The new scheme retains the industrial awareness but has a much lighter and more fluid feel. It has at its centre a favourite Duffy concept, 'the club' – a place for nomadic workers to meet colleagues and visitors or to sit and read, preparing themselves for a meeting or presentation.

This mobile environment contrasts with the permanence of an assigned workstation for support staff, either in administrative, financial or document management functions. In between these two extremes are the so-called 'team residents' – people who are assigned to a project team for a period that can range from three weeks to a year. They work in one of seven project team areas which have been specifically designed to support team activities.

The management of such flexible environments is important and facilities management guidelines have been put into place. These include a 'clear desk' policy and technology provision – a cordless office telephone handset for people to use around the office as well as docking ports for laptop computers.

At DEGW, an individual can choose whether to find an area for concentration and privacy or to be a part of an interactive hub that encourages collaboration. The new scheme results in a higher proportion of total floor space that is given over to support facilities rather than owned workspaces, but it is work in these central, shared areas that stimulates the interaction through which architectural ideas and creativity emerge.

location
london, UK

client
DEGW

completed
1997

total floor space
1,331 square metres
(14,325 square feet)

staff
106 people

cost
£450,000

1

1 The main 'club' area
provides a shared
environment for nomadic
workers to use. Cordless
office telephones,
shown here on a central
recharging rack, provide
the technology for mobile
working.

1 Floor plan showing:

■ Bookable
1 Study booth
2 Quiet room
3 Meeting room 3
4 Meeting room 4
5 Meeting room 5
6 Meeting room 6
7 Meeting room 7
8 Open study
9 Independent area

■ Support
17 The pick-up zone
18 Fax/mail area
19 Document centre
20 Sample library
21 Preparation area
22 Training area

■ Touchdown
10 Knowledge centre
11 Study booths
12 The club
13 The hub
14 The heritage area

■ Homebases
15 Administrative support
16 Project teams

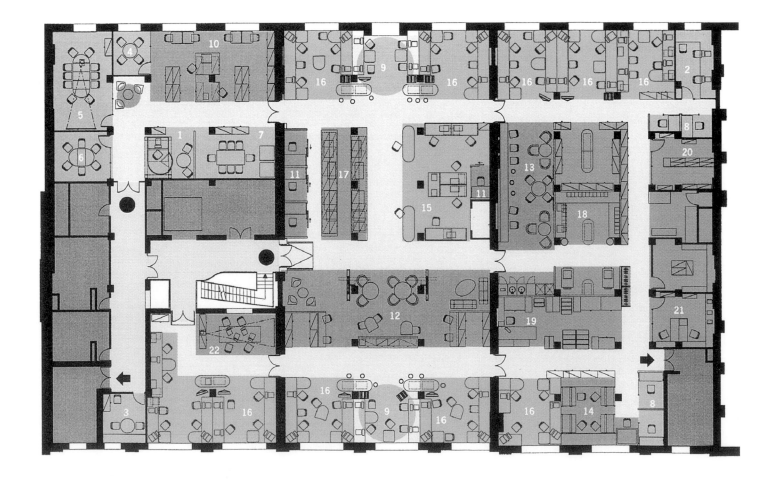

2

2 Within the touchdown
   zone, the hub provides
   a place for informal
   meetings or access
   to information through
   shared computers
   located along the
   raised workbench.

innsbruck alpine school   PETER LORENZ

THE final project in this book is perhaps the ultimate mobile workplace: the 'Office Box' espouses the concept of work anywhere by placing this 'container office' in an Austrian woodland, a functional interface between the world of work and the natural world. The Sylvan Urbanity project, an organizer of mountain climbing tours, sets out to combine a work environment with the product itself – a love of the great outdoors.

On entering the container cubes through a glazed bridge from the main office building, the first impression is of a conventional office with desks and conference tables. But architect Peter Lorenz has created a glass façade covering the entire east side of the building that creates a sense of openness and makes the occupants feel that they are physically inside the surrounding woods.

The perceived seclusion hides the interactive nature of the rooms themselves, with high ceilings and creative lighting providing an effective work environment for team meetings or briefings. The metal staircase that seems to float freely, connecting the buildings with the surrounding woodland, completes the symbiosis.

The concept shows that the boundaries of future work do not end at the four walls of the average office building. Work is beginning to transcend the physical barriers of man-made buildings as technology and work patterns change the preconceived ideas of location and place. With its integration of inner and outer office space, the Office Box points to a future workplace that will meet the needs of an increasingly mobile and transient workforce – and draw directly on natural references all around.

location
natters, austria

client
innsbruck alpine school/hannes gasser

completed
spring 1996

total floor space
110 square metres
(1,200 square feet)

staff
14 people

cost
£310,500

1

2

1   The distinctions between
    inside and outside are
    blurred through the use
    of full height glazing.

2   Deep in an alpine forest
    the world of work
    communes with nature.

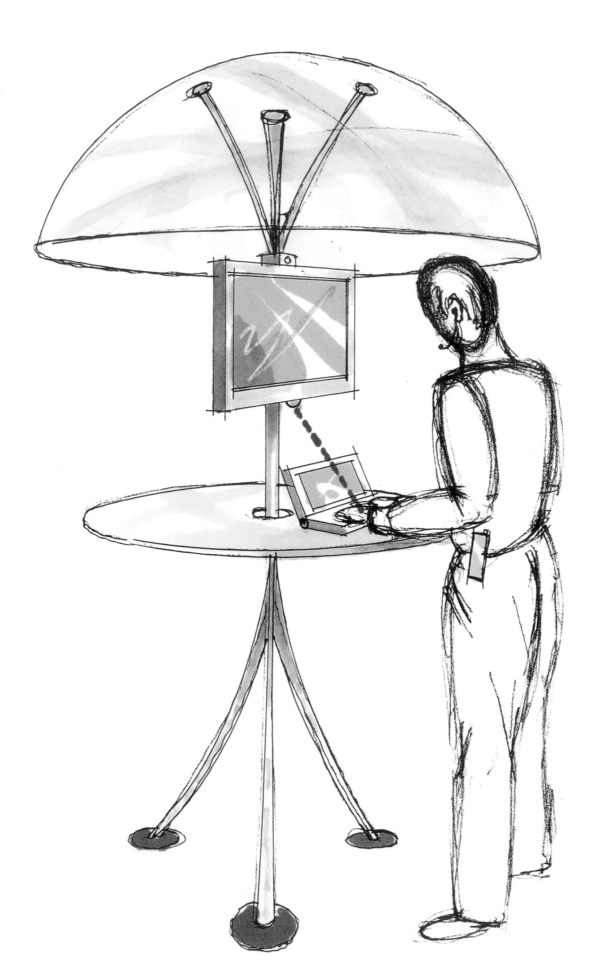

Knowlegible future
workspace:

1 Knowledge exchange
2 Lay-by
3 Touchdown
4 Open plan
5 Project/client rooms
6 Cellular
7 Modules
8 Formal meeting
9 Breakout space
10 Informal meeting
11 Food and drink
12 Relax area
13 Gym
14 Shopping

booz allen & hamilton dome pod

MATTHEW CALVERT AND PHILIP ROSS

THIS concept was originally developed by architect Matthew Calvert and consultant Philip Ross for use by management consultants Booz Allen & Hamilton in its offices worldwide. It is a touchdown station for the mobile worker who just wants to 'touch base' with the organization for a short period of time. Its plexiglass dome (see left) gives acoustic privacy within an open-plan environment while a flatscreen built into a central column connects the laptop-toting user to the corporate network through an infra-red link. Together with the mobile worker's cordless office telephone, the Dome Pod provides an abbreviated workstation offering all connections during a temporary stay. Within an office dedicated to mobility (the 'Knowlegible' future workspace created for the same client uses a range of cordless technologies), the Dome Pod would sit in a lay-by area of the open-plan space (below).

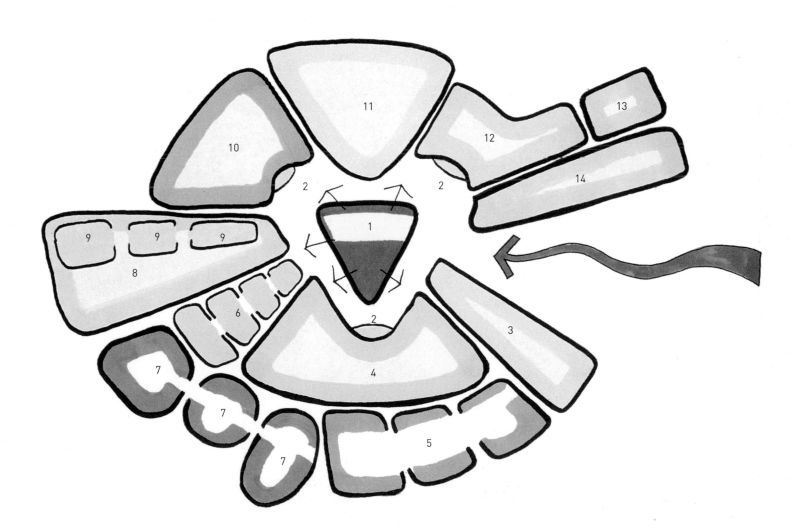

BIOGRAPHIES

Apicella Associates
9 Ivebury Court, 325 Latimer Road, London W10 6RA, UK

Apicella Associates Ltd, formerly Apicella Associates Architecture and Design, London, was founded by Lorenzo Apicella in 1989. Apicella studied architecture at Nottingham University, Canterbury College of Art and the Royal College of Art in London before moving to the United States to work for Skidmore, Owings and Merrill. From 1986 to 1989 he was head of the architecture and interior design group Imagination Design & Communications, collaborating with such clients as Harrods, British Telecom, Forte Plc, Ford and British Steel. Lorenzo Apicella currently serves on the RIBA Awards Panel, has been chairman of the National Awards jury four times and most recently served as an international juror for the American Institute of Architects Awards in San Diego. He has taught widely within the UK and has been visiting critic at Canterbury, London and Oxford. Apicella Associates' current projects range across the full spectrum of design from furniture to urban planning.

Baum Thornley Architects
340 Bryant Street # 300a, San Francisco, CA 94107, USA

Baum Thornley Architects are active in the fields of architecture and interior design, real estate feasibility analysis and construction administration. The practice was founded by Robert Baum and Douglas Thornley and today works on a number of project types – offices, retail, civic centres, medical, biotechnical facilities, warehouse conversions, industrial schemes and residences.

BDG/McColl
24 St John Street, London EC1M 4AY, UK

BDG/McColl (formerly the Business Design Group) was founded in 1962. Specializing in office planning and design, they have offices throughout the UK and also in Frankfurt and Budapest. Clients BDG have worked with include Thomas Cook, American Express, Inland Revenue, Department of Trade and Industry, Department of the Environment, Department of Transport, British Gas, Ernst and Young, Smith Kline Beecham and BZW. The practice is split into four sectors each cornering different areas of the marketplace. 'BDG McColl Architecture' deals with the design of shopping centres, offices and manufacturing facilities, 'BDG McColl Communications' with graphic design and brand identities as well as staff communications, 'BDG McColl Retail and Leisure' with the development of brand strategy and design of retail and leisure environments whereas 'BDG McColl Workplace' offers a service in the space planning, design and construction management of workplace environments.

Behnisch, Behnisch & Partner
Büro Innenstadt, Christophstrasse 6, Stuttgart D–70178, Germany

Günter Behnisch was born in Dresden in 1922. He studied at the Technical University of Stuttgart and set up his own office in 1952. In 1979 he founded Behnisch & Partner with Winfried Buxel, Manfred Sabatke and Erhard Tranker. Today the firm has two offices, Behnisch & Partner and Behnisch, Behnisch & Partner and has taken on two further partners, Stefan Behnisch and Günter Schaller. Both practices concentrate on large-scale public commissions. Recent projects include banks in Frankfurt, Munich and Stuttgart; school sports facilities and the German Flight Safety Bureau. Behnisch is a member of the Akademie der Künste, an Honorary Doctor at the University of Stuttgart, a member of the International Academy of Architecture in Sofia and an honorary member of the Royal Incorporation of Architects in Scotland. In 1992 he was awarded the Gold Medal by the Architecture Academy in Paris.

Mario Bellini Associati Srl
Piazza Arcole 4, Milan 20143, Italy

Mario Bellini studied at the Milan Polytechnic. Editor of *Domus* from 1986 to 1991, he has lectured at leading design schools throughout the world and since 1995 has taught at the University of Genoa School of Architecture. Completed projects include the office building of the AEM Thermoelectric Power Plant at Cassano d'Adda, the Milan Trade Fair Extension, the Tokyo Design Centre, the Schmidtbank Headquarters in Germany, the new Arsoa Company Headquarters in Yamanashi-ken, and the Natuzzi Americas Inc. Headquarters in North Carolina. Bellini is also well known for his exhibition design working on shows such as 'The Treasury of San Marco in Venice' at the Grand Palais in Paris. Bellini has been involved in product and furniture design since 1963; examples of his products can be seen in design collections including that of the Museum of Modern Art in New York.

Abe Bonnema
Bureau for Architecture and Environmental Planning BV, Postbus 15, 9254 ZV, Hardgarijp, Holland, The Netherlands

Abe Bonnema's earliest designs are to be found in Leeuwarden and include the Girobank Building, offices for the municipal social services and for the insurance companies Avero and FBTO. He is best known for his design of the Head Office of the Nationale Nederlanden in Rotterdam which, at 150 metres high, is the tallest building in The Netherlands.

Buschow Henley
21 Little Portland Street, London W1N 5AF, UK

Buschow Henley was established in November 1994 by Ralph Buschow and Simon Henley with Ken Rorrison and Gavin Hale Brown joining as partners the following year. Buschow studied at the University of Manitoba and the Architectural Association and worked for various firms such as Harper Mackay and Herron Associates before setting up his own studio. Simon Henley graduated from the Universities of Liverpool and of Oregon and is currently undertaking an M.Phil. at the Bartlett School. Prior to forming his collaboration with Buschow he also worked for Harper Mackay as well as Lifshutz Davidson amongst others. The practice is involved with residential, workplace, health, education and exhibition design projects. Their clients include University College, London; Mazda; the RAC; Wolff Olins; Sony Music; L'Ouverture Theatre Company and the Manhattan Loft Corporation. Buschow and Henley's work has been the subject of numerous articles and has been featured on TV and radio.

Matthew Calvert and Philip Ross
195 London Road, Twickenham, Middlesex TW1 1EJ and 152 Iverson Road, London NW6 2HH, UK respectively

Matthew Calvert is an architect specializing in creative solutions for business and commercial interiors. Completed projects include recording studios and workplaces for media companies, banking institutions and corporate headquarters. He graduated from Kingston Polytechnic in 1983 and worked for a number of leading architectural firms prior to setting up his own practice in 1997. Together with workplace consultant Philip Ross, he has developed innovative future workplace concepts that illustrate how new technologies will change the way we work.

CD Partnership
22 Shad Thames, London SE1 2YU, UK

The architecture, interior and graphic design practice, CD Partnership, was founded by Terence Conran and today employs over 20 designers and architects. Recent projects include the design of the Longman Publishing Group's new headquarters in Harlow, Essex; the Conran restaurant Mezzo; the café and lido on two levels of Celebrity Cruises' new super liner launched in 1995; the Triest Hotel in Vienna, Selfridges' restaurant, Quaglino's restaurant and various office schemes including the headquarters for Godman. Graphic design projects include the full design and implementation of the new corporate identity for Cabouchon, the UK's leading fashion jeweller, and a development programme for Providence Capitol's product literature.

DEGW
8 Crinan Street, London N1 9SQ, UK

DEGW was established in 1973 by Francis Duffy, John Worthington and Luigi Giffone as an architectural and space-planning firm. It is a major European concern with offices in Manchester, Glasgow, Madrid, Milan, Paris, Amersfoort, Brussels, Berlin and Munich. Clients include British Nuclear Fuel, IBM UK, Christie's London, Lloyds Bank and Olivetti. The firm has won numerous major competitions including one to design a large industrial development in Wedding, Berlin. DEGW has published its ideas on office planning in various publications, most notably in *Planning Office Space* by Duffy, Worthington and DEGW's Managing Director Colin Cave, and in Duffy's *The Changing Workplace*. They have also carried out many multi-client studies on the impact of information technology on office buildings, including the Workplace Forum Research Programme.

Fernau & Hartman Architects
2512 Ninth Street No. 2, Berkeley, CA 94710, USA

Fernau & Hartman was founded in 1980 by Richard Fernau (b. 1946) and Laura Hartman (b. 1952). They both have Masters of Architecture degrees from the University of California, Berkeley, where they teach today. Fernau worked as art director with Jonathan Demme at New World Pictures in Hollywood and for the architect Steiger Partner Architekten in Zurich before opening his own practice and eventually going into partnership. Hartman worked with several architectural practices in the USA and Switzerland and is also a painter who has exhibited her work both nationally and internationally. Together they have received awards for all their built projects and have earned reputations for their architectural design, interior design and technical innovation. Their work ranges from furniture and interiors to residential, commercial and institutional buildings. Recent schemes include the Von Stein Residence, collective housing for the Cheesecake Consortium, the Tipping Building, the f/X Networks Corporate Headquarters and the Nickelodeon Headquarters. Their work has been published both nationally and internationally.

Sir Norman Foster and Partners
Riverside Three, 22 Hester Road, London SW11 4AN, UK

Sir Norman Foster was born in Manchester, England in 1935 and studied architecture and city planning at the University of Manchester and at Yale University. He established Team 4 in 1963 – with his late wife, Wendy, and Su and Richard Rogers – and founded Foster Associates in 1967. Today he is internationally famous for his high-tech designs, many of which, such as the Hong Kong and Shanghai Bank (1979–86), and Stansted Airport (1981–89) have resulted directly from competitions. Projects include the Sackler Galleries at the Royal Academy of Arts, London, which was named the RIBA building of the year in 1993; the Centre d'Art/Cultural Centre, Nimes; the ITN Headquarters, London; Cranfield University Library; the new wing of the Joslyn Art Museum in Omaha, Nebraska, and the Cambridge University Law Faculty. Master plans include the King's Cross development and complete projects number the Reichstag remodelling, Berlin and an airport at Chek Lap Kok for Hong Kong – covering an area of 1,248 hectares (3,084 acres), this is the largest project in the world. Foster received a knighthood in the Queen's Birthday Honours in 1991, and his work has won over 60 awards and citations. He is a well-known figure on the international lecturing circuit. Although primarily concerned with large-scale architectural projects, Foster is also involved in furniture design.

Harper Mackay Architects
33–37 Charterhouse Square, London EC1M 6AE, UK

Harper Mackay works predominantly in the world of architecture and interiors. It was established in 1987 by David Harper and Ken Mackay. Clients number BP and the Virgin Group and current and recent projects include Ian Schrager Hotels, offices for McCann Erickson, M&C Saatchi, BP, Central Television, fX Center and ONdigital.

Kunihiko Hayakawa Architect and Associates
Yoga A-Flat 707 3-1-17, Kamiyoga, Setagaya-ku, Tokyo 158-0098, Japan

Kunihiko Hayakawa was born in Tokyo in 1941. He received his Bachelor of Architecture from the Waseda University and went on to study for a Masters in Environmental Design which he received from Yale University in 1971. He worked for Moshe Safdie and Associates in Montreal before establishing his own practice in 1978. He has taught at the School of Architecture in Washington University, at the Japan AIR project, Rotterdam and at the Waseda University, Musashino Insitute of Art. Hayakawa has received many awards for his work, most recently first

prize in the design competition for the Kirishima Art Hall and the Togo Murano Award for his design of the Park Court in Suginami-Miyamae.

Heikkinen-Komonen Architects
Kristianinkatu 11–13, Helsinki 00170, Finland

Heikkinen-Komonen Architects was founded in 1974 by Mikko Heikkinen (b. 1949) and Markku Komonen (b. 1945) who both received Masters degrees from Helsinki University of Technology in 1974 and worked for various architectural practices within Finland before forming their partnership. Heikkinen has held teaching posts at Helsinki University and in 1922 was given a New York residence scholarship by the Finnish Foundation of Visual Arts. He is a visiting critic at the Philadelphia College of Textiles and Science; University College, Dublin; the University of Virginia and the Stadelschule, Frankfurt. Komonen has been the Professor of Architecture at Helsinki University of Technology since 1992 as well as visiting teacher at the University of Houston (1983–93). He was also the Editor-in-Chief of *Arkkitechi* magazine (1977–80) and Director of the Exhibition Department of the Museum of Finnish Architecture (1978–86). The practice's early projects include renovations and retail and exhibition designs in Finland, but in the 1990s the practice undertook increasingly large commissions both nationally and internationally such as Heureka Science centre, near Helsinki; Rovaniemi Airport; the European Film College in Ebeltoft, Denmark; a Health Unit in Guinea, Africa; fair pavilions for Marimekko in Düsseldorf, Frankfurt, Copenhagen and Paris; and the Finnish embassies in Washington and Berlin.

Helin & Siitonen Architects
PO Box 502, Helsinki HN 00101, Finland

Helin & Siitonen was founded in 1979 work undertaken since then has ranged from summer cottages to corporate headquarters and master plans for mixed use developments. The practice specializes in cultural institutions, offices, commercial and recreational developments and housing.

Hellmuth, Obata + Kassabaum (HOK) Inc.
One Metropolitan Square, 211 North Broadway, St Louis, Missouri 63102–2231, USA

Hellmuth, Obata & Kassabaum was founded in 1955 and today employs over 1,300 people. Their area of expertise covers work for major corporations, developers, state and local agencies, sports facilities, hospitals, colleges and universities, the US government and governments in Canada, the Caribbean, Central and South America, the Middle East and Asia. The firm offers services in architecture, engineering, interior design, graphic design, planning, landscape architecture, facility programming/management and consulting. Gyo Obata FAIA, is co-chairman of the firm. He received a Bachelors degree in architecture in 1945 from Washington University and a Masters in architecture and urban design from the Cranbrook Academy of Art. He has Honorary Ph.D.s from Washington and the University of Missouri. George Hellmuth (now retired) received a Bachelors and Masters degree from Washington University and also studied at the Ecole des Beaux Arts at Fountainebleau, France. He was given the Gold Medal Award by the St Louis chapter of the AIA. George Kassabaum FAIA (died 1982) also studied at Washington University. He served as a national president of the AIA (1968–69) and as chancellor of the College of Fellows of the AIA (1977–78). HOK's major recent projects include the Federal Reserve Bank in Minneapolis; the Los Angeles County Replacement Hospital; the Department of State US Embassy in Moscow, and a high-rise for the Principal Life Insurance Company in Des Moines, Iowa.

Holey Associates
2 South Park, Floor 3, San Francisco, CA 94107, USA

Holey Associates was founded in 1984 and has created workplaces for companies such as Monsanto, CBS Television, CUC International Robertson Stephens/Bank of America and Andersen Consulting and also for younger cutting edge enterprises including Idea Factory, Wired Ventures, Revo Sunglasses and Univision Television Group. Holey Associates works throughout the United States and the company's designs, commentary and forecasts concerning the changing workplace have appeared frequently in leading national and international design publications.

IDEO Product Design and Development
7/8 Jeffreys Place, Jeffreys Street, London NW1 9PP, UK

IDEO is an international product design and development consultancy. It developed from Moggridge Associates, an industrial design consultancy founded in 1969. Ten years later a second office was opened in California's Silicon Valley which led to a growing interest in design user interfaces and software. Varying facilities were added to the company throughout the 1980s and 1990s and IDEO itself was formed in 1991 when David Kelley Design and Matrix Design merged to provide a full service product development group with offices in London, Boston, Chicago, San Francisco and Palo Alto. Further branches have since been opened in Tokyo, Grand Rapids, Milan and Tel Aviv. In 1996 IDEO was voted

'Design Group of the Year' by Design Zentrum in Essen, Germany. Today clients include the BBC, Apple, NEC, Nike, Nokia, Samsung, Siemens and Warner Bros and the practice has been responsible for the creation of over 2,000 complex medical, computer, telecommunications, industrial and consumer products and has led the way in the new discipline of interaction design.

Daryl Jackson
35 Little Bourke Street, Melbourne, Victoria 3000, Australia

Daryl Jackson has offices in Melbourne, Sydney, Canberra and Brisbane and international branches in London and Berlin. In London the practice has recently built a series of insertions into the existing railway arches underneath Cannon Street Station creating the 'Cannons Health Club'. Other leisure projects include the Welsh Garden Festival Pavilion and the Cedars Health and Leisure Club in Richmond which received the RIBA regional award. They have also completed various housing projects along the Thames for the London Docklands Authority ranging from an adaptive re-use of redundant warehousing to a new wall of housing near Tower Bridge. Daryl Jackson has undertaken a heritage redevelopment office project in Budapest, housing and offices in Potsdam and has won a housing/urban planning competition in Brandenberg. The office in Berlin is currently documenting a major residence in Berlin and exploring a redevelopment housing study for the site of the 1936 Olympic Games Village.

Jestico + Whiles Architects
14 Stephenson Way, London NW1 2HD, UK

The architectural practice of Jestico + Whiles was founded in 1977 by principals Tom Jestico, John Whiles, Robert Collingwood and Tony Ingram and today has offices in London, Glasgow, Prague and Munich. Preoccupation with lightweight structures and components can be seen in early industrial projects at Epsom (1979) and Waltham Cross (1982), while later schemes for Friends of the Earth, the Policy Studies Institute and research for the UK Department of Energy represent the development of Jestico & Whiles's approach to the concept of low-energy workspaces. Further projects include a science and technology park in Scotland and several inner-city industrial/office buildings, including Gallery Court, Stukeley Street and Jockey's Fields. Current work numbers embassies and ambassador's residences in Latvia and Bulgaria; a major CrossRail station interchange; two hotels in central London; and their largest project to date – Burrell's Wharf, a £28 million residential and leisure development on a Grade II-listed site in London's docklands.

Eva Jiricna Architects Ltd
Sun Court House, 18–26 Essex Road, London N1 8LN, UK

Eva Jiricna studied architecture at the Engineer University of Prague and went on to complete a postgraduate degree in fine art at the Prague Academy. She moved to the UK in the late 1960s and became Dip. Arch. of the Royal Institute of British Architects. Unable to return to Czechoslovakia following the events of 1968 she worked for a series of British architectural practices including a short period with Sir Richard Rogers where she was involved as team leader for the interior design of the new Lloyds Headquarters. She formed her own practice in 1984 and quickly developed an international reputation with clients such as Joseph, Vitra and Legends nightclub. She has been associated with staircases since the celebrated glass and steel versions she designed for Joseph and Joan & David Inc. in the USA and Europe and in 1994 a study of this subject won the Design Prize in the Royal Academy Summer Show. Jiricna has built up long-standing relationships with clients such as Andersen Consulting for which she has completed flagship headquarters in the Gehry building in Prague. She is also working for the London Docklands Development Committee and is currently involved in the design of the Soul Zone or 'Spirit Level' in the Millennium Dome, Greenwich. Eva Jiricna has been the recipient of numerous honours in the UK and Prague. She is an Honorary Fellow of the Royal College of Art and in 1991 was designated a Royal Designer for Industry by the Royal Society of Arts. She is also a member of the Prague Presidential Council and was made a CBE (Commander of the British Empire) for services to design. Most recently she has been elected to the Royal Academy of Arts as an Academician. She has taught and lectured throughout the UK and held architectural workshops for the Universities of Harvard and Pennsylvania.

Kauffmann Theilig & Partner
Zeppelinstrasse 10, Ostildern 73760, Stuttgart, Germany

Dieter Kauffmann was born in 1954 in Sindelfingen. After graduating from the Fachhochschule of Augsburg in 1978, he worked for architects in Stuttgart before taking up an appointment with Behnisch and Partner in 1980 where he remained until he joined Heinle, Wischer and Partner. In 1988, he went into partnership with Andreas Theilig. Theilig was born in Stuttgart in 1951. After graduating from the Technische Hochschule in Darmstadt in 1978 he worked briefly for architects in Darmstadt before also joining Behnisch and Partner. He has lectured at the Fachhochschule in Biberach.

Ben Kelly Design

10 Stoney Street, London SE1 9AD, UK

Ben Kelly Design was established in London in
1977 by designer Ben Kelly (b. 1949), who studied
environmental/interior design at the Royal College
of Art, graduating in 1974. Elena Massucco joined
the practice in 1987 and Chris Cawte in 1991; key
designers who have worked for BKD include
Sandra Douglas and Peter Mance; all four are
graduates of Kingston University's interior design
course. Kelly's early individual projects include
the Howie Shop (1977); work for Malcolm
McLaren/The Sex Pistols; and Lynne Frank's
first office. BKD's major designs number
the Hacienda nightclub and venue, Manchester;
the 4AD record company headquarters, London;
and offices for Rainey Kelly Campbell Roalfe
advertising agency, London, as well as new offices
for Lynne Frank. BKD have also worked on the
exhibition design for the 1996 BBC Design Awards
and the Glasgow International Festival of Design
1996 Exhibition. Recently they also worked on a
flagship store scheme for a major clothing
company. Kelly has taught interior/3D design at
Kingston University and acts as external assessor
at Glasgow School of Arts. *Plans and Elevations*, a
book on the practice, was published in 1990
and BKD featured in 'Sublime: The Sol Mix', an
exhibition, Kelvingrove Art Gallery, Glasgow (1992).
The practice has won numerous awards for 'The
Basement' in the Science Museum, London and
has received much acclaim for the British Design
Council offices in London.

LOG ID

Sindelfinger Strasse 85, Glashaus, Tubingen
72070, Germany

LOG ID is a team of botanists, doctors, physicists,
communication psychologists and architects who
work together to solve problems of environmental
design. The theoretical foundation of their practice
is 'green solar architecture' which they achieve by
the construction of sophisticated glass-house
constructions which combine technological and
economic planning with the human need for high
living standards. In addition to private homes, LOG
ID design factories, hospitals and public office
buildings.

Peter Lorenz

Maria Theresien Strasse 37, Innsbruck A–6020,
Austria

Peter Lorenz was born in Innsbruck in 1950 and
received a Masters degree in architecture from the
University of Venice. He has had his own practice
since 1980 and today has offices in Innsbruck
and Vienna. He has completed over 200 projects
ranging from housing schemes, retail outlets and
offices and has recently undertaken city planning

and large urban schemes. He is a lecturer at
various universities and frequently holds
workshops and study trips worldwide.

Mahmoudieh Design

Pestalozzi Strasse 99A, 10625 Berlin, Germany

Yasmine Mahmoudieh was born in Germany. She
studied Art History in Florence, Architecture at the
Ecole D'Ingenieur in Geneva, Interior Design at the
College of Notre Dame in Belmont as well as
Architecture and Interior Design at the University
of California in Los Angeles where she received
her Diploma. She worked for various architectural
practices in the States before co-founding The
Architectural Design Group International in 1986,
followed by her own company based in Los
Angeles. Today Mahmoudieh Design has offices in
Hamburg and Berlin and is due to open a branch
in London. Mahmoudieh designs restaurants,
exhibition and fair stands, boarding houses and
furniture. She also undertakes the interior design
of hotels and office buildings. Selected projects
include the Kempinski Hotel, Bad Saarow,
Germany; the Millennium Centre in Budapest,
Hungary; offices for Garbe KG in Hamburg,
Germany; 'The Factory' in East Berlin (conversion
of an old mill into galleries, restaurants, offices
and lofts); the Gordon Eckhard Production Studios
in Hollywood; and the renovation of a former
Beatles' house, De La Bruyere-Residence in
Beverly Hills.

Martorell-Bohigas-Mackay

Placa Reial 18, Pral., Barcelona 08002, Spain

Josep Martorell and Oriol Bohigas studied
together before founding MBM in 1951. David
Mackay joined the partnership in 1962 and Albert
Puig Domenech in 1986. Martorell was head of the
architectural department of the Vila Olimpica,
guiding the urban design of the scheme. Bohigas
was in charge of the Barcelona School of
Architecture from 1977 to 1980, at which time he
became chief architect and planner of the first
democratic government of the city. With a staff
of around 25 the firm has handled over 300
architecture and urban planning and design
schemes during the last 40 years, working in
Mexico, France, Germany, The Netherlands, Italy,
Scotland and Wales. Projects include the Olympic
Village and Olympic Port in Barcelona and the
main pavilion for Expo '92 Seville; housing in
Breda, The Netherlands (1995); Bite Avenue and
Square in Cardiff (1994); urban-design studies for
Edinburgh waterfront (1995); and urban-planning
studies with new photovoltaic/thermal building
components for the Directorate General, Science
Research and Development – European
Commission (1995). The practice has taken part in
numerous international competitions, frequently
being awarded first prize.

Atelier Mendini Srl

Via Sannio 24, Milan 20137, Italy

Alessandro Mendini was born in 1931 in Milan
where he later studied architecture at the
polytechnic. He has been editor of the design
magazines *Casabella*, *Modo* and *Domus* as well
as directing the journal *Ollo*. For many years he
has been the theorist of avant-garde design, co-
founding the Global Tools Group in 1973 as a
counter-movement to established Italian design.
In 1978 he started his collaboration with Studio
Alchimia in Milan and evolved the so-called 'banal
design' which sought to change items in daily use
into new and ironical objects – a notable example
is the early version of the Proust Chair painted in
a divisionist technique for the Bauhaus Collection
in 1980. In 1983 he became Professor of Design at
the University of Applied Art in Vienna and was
also made a member of the scientific committee
of the Domus Academy. In the late 1980s he
established the Genetic Laboratory for Visual
Surprises in order to research and question
established ideas of taste and form. His work
covers architecture, furniture, product, tableware
and interior design and he is currently design
advisor for Swatch and Alessi, amongst others.
Additional clients include Zanotta, Fiat, Zabro,
Driade, Poltronova, Elam and Abet Laminati. In
1990 he set up Atelier Mendini with his brother
Francesco Mendini designing projects such as the
Groningen Museum and, with Yumiko Kobayashi,
the Paradise Tower, Hiroshima. Alessandro
Mendini's work has been the subject of countless
exhibitions and one-man shows worldwide.

Morphosis

2041 Colorado Avenue, Santa Monica, CA 904041,
USA

Morphosis was founded in 1972 by Thom Mayne
and Jim Stafford. Currently the office employs
approximately 20 architects and designers directed
by Thom Mayne, John Enright and Kim Groves.
Mayne graduated from the University of Southern
California in 1968 and set up a collaborative,
Southern California Institute of Architecture. He
received his Masters from Harvard ten years later
and in 1987 received the Rome Prize Fellowship
from the American Academy in Rome. He has
taught throughout the States including Columbia
University as well as at the Berlage Institute
in The Netherlands and the Bartlett School of
Architecture in London. He is currently lecturing
at the UCLA School of Arts and Architecture.
Morphosis have won various international design
competitions, three of which are under
construction. They have been the recipient of 16
Progressive Architecture Awards, 27 AIA awards
and have participated in numerous group and solo
exhibitions including a major retrospective which
took place in Madrid in 1998.

Toru Murakami Architect and Associates

1–27 Hijiyamahommachi, Ninami, Hiroshima, 732–0816, Japan

Toru Murakami was born in Imabari, Ehime Prefecture and graduated from the architecture department of the Hiroshima Institute of Technology. For the following three years he worked for the Shozo Uchii Architectural Design Office, opening his own practice in 1976. From 1992 he has been the Affiliated Professor at the School of Engineering in the Hiroshima Institute of Technology. Murakami has been honoured on numerous occasions within his country and in 1994 was the recipient of the Architectural Institute of Japan Design Prize for a series of housing projects including a house in Ajina.

Cesar Pelli and Associates Inc.

1056 Chapel Street, New Haven, CT 06510, USA

Cesar Pelli founded his own company in 1977, after a career which had seen, amongst other projects, the construction of the Pacific Design Centre in Los Angeles and the US Embassy in Tokyo, and his appointment as Dean of the Yale University School of Architecture. Born in Argentina, and trained at the University of Tucuman, Pelli came to the States with a scholarship to attend the University of Illinois. His belief that buildings should be 'responsible citizens' is reflected in his concern for their suitability in terms of locations and the city skyline. His first project after 1977 was the expansion and renovation of the Museum of Modern Art in New York; the company has since received over 80 awards for design excellence, including an AIA citation for the World Financial Centre and Winter Garden at Battery Park city, which was cited as being one of the ten best works of architecture completed after 1980. The AIA also awarded Cesar Pelli and Associates the 1989 Firm Award in recognition of over a decade of leading-edge work in architectural design. Pelli himself was given the AIA 1995 Gold Medal which honours a lifetime of distinguished achievements and outstanding contributions.

Powell-Tuck Associates

14 Barley Mow Passage, Chiswick, London W4 4PH, UK

Powell-Tuck Associates is a design practice specializing in architecture, interior design, furniture design, product design and hard landscaping and is predominantly involved with refurbishment and speculative office and shop space. Their concern is to make existing buildings work in contemporary society. Julian Powell-Tuck graduated from the Royal College of Art in London in 1976 with a Masters Degree in Environmental Design. He founded his own practice the same year in partnership with David Connor and Gunnar Orefelt and continued to receive international acclaim. He also set up an office in Taiwan to accommodate the increasing workload from the Far East. Powell-Tuck Associates was formed in 1990. Julian Powell-Tuck lectures widely within the UK and is currently lecturer in Architecture and Interior Design at the Royal College of Art. He is also an external examiner at Leeds University.

Samyn and Partners

Chée de/Stwg op Waterloo, 1537, Brussels B–1180, Belgium

Samyn and Partners was founded in 1980 by Philippe Samyn and reorganized in 1991 to include associates Richard Delaunoit and Denis Melotte. The firm is active in the fields of research and development, planning, landscape design, architecture and interior design, and has undertaken work in The Netherlands, England, Spain, France, Greece and Italy as well as in Belgium. Projects include the National Bank of Belgium, Brussels (1981–84); the Thompson Aircraft Tire Corporation Frameries (1991); the renovation of the Solboch University Campus, Brussels; and M & G Richerche SpA Vanafro, Italy (1990–91), as well as numerous town-planning and housing schemes. Philippe Samyn was born in 1948 and studied at the Massachusetts Institute of Technology and at the Ecole de Commerce, Solvay. He has been Principal Lecturer at the Free University of Brussels in the Faculty of Applied Sciences since 1984 and at the National School of Architecture, La Cambre, since 1978. In 1992 Samyn was elected as corresponding member of the Royal Academy of Belgium and member of the board of SECO (National Technical Control Office for Construction).

Sedley Place

68 Venn Street, London SW4 0AX, UK

Sedley Place is an international design firm with offices in New York and Berlin. They are a multi-disciplinary team of interior, graphic and product designers specializing in corporate communication, brand development and packaging as well as interior design and architecture. Projects include brochures and interiors for the Gleneagles Hotel; the refurbishment of London houses including that of the film director Ridley Scott; the design and implementation of interiors for the advertising agency Lowe Group worldwide (in particular their flagship in London); and the headquarters of EMI Records, also in London. They have designed corporate identities for Volkswagen AG, the Grand Metropolitan Plc, Alfred McAlpine and Trafalgar House as well as designing branding for Smirnoff Vodka, Heineken Beer and Accurist Watches.

Shubin + Donaldson

629 State Street, Santa Barbara, CA 93101, USA or 9520 Jefferson Boulevard, Culver City, CA 90232, USA

Ronald Donaldson and Russell Shubin began their collaboration in 1990 and have since worked on a series of award-winning retail stores, entertainment studios, community centres and custom residential projects. Shubin graduated in architecture from the Polytechnic University at San Luis Obispo. He also studied at the Ecole d'Art et d'Architecture in France and received a Master in Business Administration degree at National University, San Diego. He began his professional career in 1985 with Blurock Partnership in Newport Beach, California. Donaldson studied at the Southern California Institute of Architecture receiving a Masters of Architecture. Before setting up his own practice he worked for Morphosis Architects and in 1996 was named one of the top 40 architects in America under the age of 40. He is currently teaching architecture and environmental design at the University of California, Santa Barbara. Work in progress includes various private residences including one for the actor Michael Keaton, retail outlets, a Toyota showroom and the rehabilitation of an old jail building into a youth centre.

Misha Stefan

45 Hereford Road, London W2 5AH, UK

Misha Stefan is a designer whose work emulates natural forms with the relation of shape, space and colour playing a major role. He graduated from the Architectural Association in 1984 and then worked for Zaha Hadid and the practices of various architects before setting up his own office in 1996. Projects to date include the Tokio fashion shop, Mission design gallery, offices for Courtney Communications and various apartments in Bayswater, Bloomsbury and Hampstead. His range of furniture was launched in November 1998.

Studios Architecture

99 Green Street, San Francisco, CA 94111, USA

Studios Architecture was founded in 1985 by Darryl T. Roberson, Erik Sueberkrop, Gene Rae and Phillip Olson and today has offices in San Francisco, Washington, New York, London and Paris. Sueberkrop, who heads the company, was born in Hamburg and educated at the University of Cincinnati, Ohio. Main projects include a manufacturing headquarters in Dublin; a university alumni and visitor centre building for the University of California; the interiors of a showroom for the Knoll Group in Germany, conference facilities for the Société Générale, Paris, interiors for the Asia and Pacific Trade

Centre in Osaka, and the Petronas headquarters in Kuala Lumpur. Studios also designs corporate interiors for many prominent law firms, financial concerns and high-tech companies in the USA, Europe and Asia, including Apple Computer, Silicon Graphics, Arnold & Porter, and Morgan Stanley & Company. The practice has been awarded American Institute of Architects Merit Awards on numerous occasions and its work has been published in leading design magazines in Europe and the USA.

Studio BAAD

Linden Mill, Linden Road, Hebden Bridge, West Yorkshire HX7 7DN, UK

Studio BAAD was founded in 1988 by Philip Bintliff who graduated in Architecture from the University of Toronto. The practice carries out a wide range of work including commercial, industrial, healthcare, entertainment and cultural buildings. In 1991 the studio won an invited competition to design a new Accident and Emergency hospital building in Liverpool. Philip Bintliff has been a visiting critic and has lectured widely throughout the UK. His work has been published in many British and European architectural magazines including *Blueprint* and *The Architectural Review*. It has also been the subject of various joint exhibitions such as the RIBA show and seminar series at the Architectural Institute of Japan, 'Sense of Place Sense of Age – The Emerging Architecture in the UK' (1994) and the Architects' Journal Centenary Exhibition in London the following year. Bintliff has recently been the winner of architectural competitions to design a Centre for the Performing Arts in Warrington and a large urban housing scheme in Manchester.

Percy Thomas Partnership

10 Cathedral Road, Cardiff CF1 9YF, Wales, UK

Percy Thomas Partnership was founded in 1912 and today has five UK offices and associated offices in Hong Kong and Malaysia. The practice has undertaken numerous award-winning major projects throughout the world, many of which were the result of international design competitions. Work ranges from civic buildings and structures such as cathedrals, bridges, museums and performing arts buildings through to major education and healthcare projects, and commercial and retail developments.

Niels Torp

Industrigaten 59, PO Box 5387, Majorstua, Oslo 0304, Norway

Niels Torp was born in Oslo in 1940 and graduated from Trondheim University in 1964. After further scholarship studies in Helsinki and Rome he joined the family practice of Torp Torp becoming a partner in 1970 and owner/manager in 1974. The firm expanded during the 1980s and several trend-setting office projects established its reputation as one of the leading architectural companies in Norway. In 1984 Niels Torp won the competition to build the Skandinavian Air Service (SAS) headquarters in Stockholm. He has subsequently been selected to participate in various international competitions, and has given lectures and seminars throughout Scandinavia and Western Europe. Today Niels Torp employs 55 designers and projects range from small houses to large city developments. They design offices, dwellings, airports, railway stations, sports stadia, shops and hotels. Important buildings include the Data Processing Centre of all Norwegian Savings Banks in Oslo (1984); SAS headquarters (1987); the bank headquarters of Den Norske Bank, Aker Brugge (1992); Hewlett Packard Headquarters in Oslo (1993); Inmarsat Headquarters, London (1993); and the Landsforsakringar Headquarters, Uppsala (1994). Niels Torp's most recently completed project is the headquarters of British Airways in London.

John McAslan & Partners

202 Kensington Church Street, London W8 7JH, UK

John McAslan & Partners was formed in 1983 by Jamie Troughton and John McAslan. Jamie Troughton studied at Cambridge University and subsequently worked for Foster Associates and Richard Rogers and Partners. John McAslan attended Edinburgh University. After two years with Cambridge Seven Associates in Boston, he returned from America to join Richard Rogers and Partners where he worked for three years. Major projects include Design House, London; Phases I and II of the Apple UK Headquarters, Stockley Park; and the award-winning British Rail station at Redhill. John McAslan & Partners have become increasingly involved in the design of educational and museum schemes such as a new college in Kobe, Japan which was awarded the Anthology Prize by the Architectural Institute of Japan in 1993. Work is currently taking place on several major master planning, new-build and restoration projects in the UK, Europe, Bangkok and the USA. They completed the Yapi Kredi Bank Operations Centre in Turkey in 1997 and are currently working on the Cincinnati Art Museum.

Valerio Dewalt Train Associates

200 North Lasalle Street, Chicago, Illinois 60601, USA

Valerio Dewalt Train was founded over 30 years ago and deals with both new construction and renovations, specializing in corporate design, high-tech industrial buildings, laboratory and research facilities, retail schemes, cultural centres and multi-family housing. The Principal-in-Charge, Joseph M. Valerio received a Bachelor of Architecture at the University of Michigan and a Masters at UCLA. He has received numerous design awards including National AIA Honour Awards and over a dozen local AIA Awards. Most recently the firm was the recipient of the Distinguished Firm Award from the Illinois AIA. Valerio is currently serving as President of the Chicago Architectural Club and is on the board of the Contemporary Arts Council. He has been responsible for many of the company's leading projects, including the apartment blocks in Arizona and California and a 400-seat restaurant in San Francisco. He has recently been in charge of the mixed-use redevelopment of the Capitol area of Madison, Wisconsin, and has overseen the $200 million construction for US Robotic during their national and international expansion. Mark D. Dewalt studied at the University of Illinois and is currently working on a headquarters for Automatic Data Processing and a dormitory renovation at Elmhurst College. The third partner, Jack de Train, is President of Valerio Dewalt Train. He trained at the University of Illinois and at the University of Tennessee where he specialized in structural engineering. He worked for Skidmore Owings & Merrill where he was associate partner before moving to VDT. He was in charge of the interior remodelling of the John C. Kluczynski Federal Building and the construction of the five-storey office addition of US Robotics. He is a fellow of the American Institute of Architects.

Weedon Partnership

Quadrant Court, 47–48 Calthorpe Road, Edgbaston, Birmingham B15 1TH, UK

Weedon Partnerhip was founded in 1932 and is associated with the house-style of the Odeon Cinema – over 300 of which were completed by 1947. The practice is based in the Midlands, UK and is currently involved in a series of major projects for the Rover Group Ltd, Argent Developments and Opel. The practice completed the provision of architectural services for the £200 million Toyota Car Factory at Burnaston, has also carried out major projects for Glaxo Research & Development Ltd.

CREDITS

Innsbruck Alpine School
Natters, Austria

Architecture and Interior Design: Peter Lorenz
Architekt & Partner.
Client: Hannes Gasser. General Contractor: Huter
& Söhne. Planning: Peter Lorenz. Project
Management: Raimund Wulz. Structural
Consultant: Christian Aste. Lighting Design:
Concept Licht. Lighting System: Galo-Tech.

Andersen Consulting, Prague: Rasin Building
Prague, Czech Republic

Architect and Interior Designer: Eva Jiricna
Architects Ltd in association with Architectural
Associates from Prague.
Client: Andersen Consulting. Main Contractor:
Techno sro Prague. Timber Fixtures: Chantiers
Baudet, France. Lighting: Concord Lighting UK.
Audio-visual Equipment: Ave Media. Office Chairs:
Herman Miller. Armchairs: Vitra Ltd.

Arthur Andersen
London, UK

Architecture and Interior Design – Project
Partners: Arthur Andersen; BDG McColl
Workplace.
Client: Arthur Andersen Business Consulting.
Main Contractor: Overburys. Furniture Suppliers:
Coexistence, Conran Shop Contracts, SCP
Contracts, Herman Miller, Ambience, Fantoni UK,
Atrium, Viaduct. Lighting Suppliers: Light Years,
Kreon, Erco, Into Lighting Design. Fabrics: Gabriel
UK, Kvadrat. Flooring Suppliers: Karndean
International Interface Europe. Tiles: Domus Tiles
Ltd. Laminates: Perstorp, Poleyrey, Abet Laminati.
Hardware: Allgoods, Handles and Fittings Ltd.
Mirrors and Glass: Chelsea Artisans.

The Boeing Leadership Center Carriage House
St Louis, Missouri, USA

Architecture and Interior Design: Hellmuth, Obata
+ Kassabaum Inc.
Project Team: Clark Davis (Project Principal); Tom
Goulden (Project Manager); Robert Blaha (Project
Designer); Brad Blythe (Project Architect);
Michelle Ludwig (Interior Designer); Tom
Kaczkowski, Mary Jo Ward (Lighting Design); Bob
Belden; Sue Wiest (Landscape Architect); Jim
Moler (Mechanical Engineer); Nada Kiblawi, Randy
Hagemann (Electrical Engineer); Gus Zuniga,
Herm Roschen (Plumbing/Fire Protection); Art
Benkieman, Steve Crang (Structural Engineer).
Client: Boeing Company. Main Contractor: J. S.

Alberici. Furniture: Stool (Knoll), Tablet Armchair
(Brayton International), Easel/flip chart/table
system (Steelcase), Seating (Herman Miller),
Mobile Cart (Haworth), Lounge Chair
(Metropolitan), Lectern (Round Oak). Lighting:
Leocus Lighting (Pendant Lighting), Ardee Lighting
(Cabinet Light), Holophane (HID Lighting), LSI
(Track Lighting), Litecontrol (Fluorescent Lighting).
Carpet: Bentley. Mobile Wall Fabrication: Technical
Products. Wall Fabric: Carnegie.

British Airways at Waterside
Harmondsworth, UK

Architecture and Interior Design: Niels Torp
Architects.
Project Team: Kathy Tilney, Tilney Shane, Alexi
Marmott, Adrian Leeman. Client: British Airways.
Collaborating Architect: RHWL. Civil/Structural
Engineer: Büro Happold. Planning Supervisor:
Halcrow H&S Ltd. Cost Consultants: AYH
Partnership. M&E Consultants: Cundall Johnston
& Partners. Landscape Consultants: Land Use
Consultants. Concrete Contractor: O'Rourke.

Bürohaus
Gniebel, Germany

Architecture and Interior Design: Kauffmann
Theilig, Freie Architekten BDA.
Project Team: Wolfgang Kergassner (Project
Partner), Ulof Ruckert (Project Architect), Tobias
Wallisser. Client: Grundstucksgesellschaft Gniebel
GbR, Pliezhausen. Structural Engineer: Ingenieur-
büro Pfefferkorn & Partner. Energy Design:
Ingenieurbüro Transsolar, Energietechnik GmbH.
HLS Planning: Schreiber Ingenieurbüro VDI.

3Com Corporation Headquarters
Santa Clara, California, USA

Architecture and Interior Design: Studios
Architecture.
Project Team: Erik Sueberkrop (Principal-in-
Charge); Cliff Peterson (Project Director), Peter
VanDine, Todd Verwers, Jean Pascal Crouzet,
Jason Lee, Shirley Perez, Chris Mitchell, Bruce
Bradsby, Jill Ingram, Todd Aranaz. Client: 3Com
Corporation. General Contractor: Rudolph &
Sletten. Structural Engineer: Structural Design
Engineers. Mechanical/Electrical/Plumbing
Engineer: Ajmani & Pamidi Inc. Civil Engineer:
Kier & Wright. Landscape Architect: Peter Walker
William Johnson & Partners. Acoustical Engineer:
Paoletti Associates. Lighting Consultant:
Architecture & Light.

Commerzbank
Frankfurt am Main, Germany

Architects: Sir Norman Foster and Partners.
Project Team: Sir Norman Foster, Spencer

de Grey, Uwe Nienstedt, Sven Ollmann and
others. Client: Commerzbank AG. Project and
Construction Management: Nervus GmbH.
Structural Engineer: Ove Arup and Partners with
Krebs and Kiefer. Mechanical Engineering:
J. Roger Preston with Petterson and Ahrens.
Electrical Engineer: Schad and Hölzel. Quantity
Surveyor: Davis Langdon and Everest. Space
Planning: Quickborner Team. Façades, Radar,
Acoustics and Building Physics: Ingenieur Büro
Schalm (IBS). Lighting: Lichtdesign; Claude
Engle. Landscape: Sommerlad and Partners.
Graphic Design: Per Arnoldi. Steel Construction:
DSD Dillinger Stahlbau GmbH. Prefab Glass:
E-Glasbeton GmbH. Façade: Josef Gartner
& Co. Floor Covering: Hacker KG. Aerated
Concrete: Hebel Alzenau GmbH and Co. Tower
Construction/Tiling: Gebrüder H & H Hell KG.
Natural Stonework: LSI Luso Sulca International.
Masonry: Opex.

DEGW Headquarters
London, UK

Architecture, Interior Design, Space Planning,
Project Management: DEGW. Client: DEGW.
Construction Managers: Interior Plc. Concept for
Mechanical Ventilation: Roger Preston & Partners.

Design Council
London, UK

Architecture and Interior Design: Ben Kelly
Design.
Project Team: Ben Kelly (Design Director), Patrick
McKinney (Project Co-ordinator/Designer),
Richard Blurton, Kevin Brennan, Chris Cawte,
Nick Toft. Client: Design Council. Main Contractor:
Billfinger and Berger UK Ltd. M/E Contractor:
Platt and Davies Electrical Contractors Ltd.
Quantity Surveyor: M. Porter Associates.
Structural Engineer: Dewhurst Macfarlane &
Partners. M/E Consultants: Fulcrum Consulting.

Discovery Channel Latin America
Miami, USA

Architecture and Interior Design: Studios
Architecture.
Project Team: Phillip Olson (Principal-in-Charge);
Yves Springuel (Project Manager); Linda Wallack
(Project Architect); Christopher Budd (Workplace
Environment Issues), Andrea Panico
(Environmental Graphics Designer), William
Deegan, Cassandra Cullison, Pablo Quintana,
Maria Pacheco. Client: Discovery Communications
Inc. Main Contractor: Skaf Construction.
Broadcast Center Contractor: Clark Construction.
Leasing Agent: The Hogan Group Inc. Broadcast
Equipment: Harris Corporation. Millwork: Bo
Childs Millwork. Acoustics Consultant: Russ
Berger Design Group. Lighting Design: Studios

Architecture. Masonry: Rover Terrazo. Tiles: Kubik Weiss. Acoustic Panels: Decoustics Quadrillon Acoustical Panels. Fabric Wrapped Acoustic Panels: Benton Brothers. Ceiling Panels: Tectum. Workstation Furniture: Haworth Crossings. Workstation Chairs: Herman Miller Aeron Chair. Conference Tables: Vecta. Lighting: Lighting Lightolier; Louis Poulsen.

Ediciones 62
Barcelona, Spain

Architecture and Interior Design: Lluis Pau/Martorell-Bohigas-Mackay.
Project Team: Mario Calavera, Alex Casas. Client: Grup 62. Master Builder: Enric Ribadulla. Builder Company: Arc 97 SL. Engineering: Albert Alentorn. Installations: Instal Ofi SA. Carpentry: Creacions Capellades SL; Tecnologias 2000 de la construccion SA. Air Conditioning: Ingenierfa y Mantenimiento SL. Painters: Decopinsa.

Fuel Design
Santa Monica, California, USA

Architecture and Interior Design: Shubin + Donaldson.
Project Team: Robin Donaldson, Russell Shubin (Principals-in-Charge); Jonathan Bloomer, Ryan Ihly. Client: Fuel Design. Contractor: LoPresti Construction.

f/X Networks Corporate Headquarters
Los Angeles, USA

Architecture and Interior Design: Fernau & Hartman Architects.
Project Team: Richard Fernau, Laura Hartman (Partners-in-Charge); Mark Macy (Project Architect); Turk Kauffmann, David Kau, Susan Stoltz (Design Team), Tom Powers, Scott Donahue, Sunshine Chen, Geoff Holton, Alice Lin, Jane Lee, Tanya Davidge. Client: f/X Networks, Fox Inc. Contractor: Gordon & Williams. Structural Engineer: John A. Martin & Asociates. Lighting: Peters & Myer Illumination Design Collaborative.

Godman
London, UK

Architecture and Interior Design: CD Partnership. Client: Godman. Main Contractor: Morgan Lovell. Lighting: Bowles Trading Co. Glass Planks: Reglit. Joinery: Morgan Lovell. Ironmongery: FSB by Allgood.

Hiratsuka Bank
Kanda, Japan

Architecture and Interior Design: Kunihiko Hayakawa Architect & Associates.

Client: Hiratsuka Bank. General Construction: Shimizu Construction Company. Consultants: Momota Structure (Structural Engineer); Go Sekkei (Mechanical Engineer).

IBM Fitout
Melbourne, Australia

Architecture and Interior Design: Daryl Jackson Pty Ltd Architects and Interior Designers. Project Team: Roman Bugryn (Project Architect); Jane Mackay, Hamish Guthrie, Casandra Hill, Steven Whiting, Paul Hecker. Client: IBM Australia. Mechanical Engineers: EMF Consultants. Electrical Engineers: Lincolne Scott Australia Pty Ltd. Specialist Lighting: Barry Webb and Associates. Quantity Surveyor: Rawlinsons.

IBM
Melbourne, Australia

Architecture and Interior Design: Daryl Jackson International.
Project Team: Daryl Jackson, Roman Bugryn, Steven Whiting, Cassandra Hill, Paul Hecker, Jane Mackay, Hamish Guthrie. Client: IBM.

IDEO San Francisco
USA

Architecture: IDEO – Project Leaders: Sam Hecht and Ian Coats MacColl. Collaborating Architect: Baum Thornley Architects.
Project Team: Douglas Thornley, Robert Baum, David Gill, Cleve Brakefield, Joseph Marshall, Douglas Diaz. Client: IDEO, San Francisco. Main Contractor: Plant Architectural Construction. Mechanical Engineer: Charles & Braun. Structural Engineer: Teyssier Engineering. Electrical Engineer: Toft.Wolff.Farrow. Lighting: Webb Design/Build.

IDEO Tokyo
Japan

Architecture: IDEO – Project Leader: Sam Hecht. Project Team: Bill Moggridge, Hideo Ottimo. Client: IDEO. Main Contractor: Sakamaki Contractors.

Independiente
London, UK

Architecture and Interior Design: Jestico + Whiles.
Client: Independiente. Main Contractor: Dawn Build. Structural Engineer: Paul Owen Associates. M&E Engineers: Peter Chittenden Associates. Reception Desk and Boardroom Table: Michael Sanders. Suppliers: Nazeing Glass (Glass Blocks); The Light Corporation; Interface (Carpets).

Interpolis
Tilburg, The Netherlands

Architecture: Bureau for Architecture and Environmental Planning BV.
Project Team: Ir. A. Bonnema b.i. Interior Designer: Kho Liang Ie Associates. Client: Interpolis. Main Contractor: Bouwcominatie BBF – Heijmans Bouw V.O.F. Layout Consultants: Veldhoen Facility Consultants BV. Landscape Architects: West 8. Consultants: Deerns Consulting Engineers BV/Technisch Adviesbureau Becks (W & E Technology), Adviesbureau Peutz & Associes BV (Building Physics), Aronshon Consulting Engineers BV (Construction), Prof Dr. W. H. Crouwel (Art). Artists: Guido Geelen, Niek Kemps.

Island Records
London, UK

Architecture and Interior Design: Powell-Tuck Associates Ltd.
Project Team: Julian Powell-Tuck, Angus Shepherd, Suzanne Smeeth, Iona Foster, Adrian Lees. Client: Island Records Ltd. Main Contractor (Phase 1): Boyle Contracts; (Phase 2): Cramb & Dean. Quantity Surveyor: Anthony J. Silver & Associates. Mechanical and Electrical Engineer: Pearce & Asociates. Structural Engineer: Whitby & Bird. Building Surveyor: Graham Cardoe & Associates. Suppliers: Concord Lighting (Lighting); Allgood (Ironmongery); Shorrock Ltd (Fire and Security); Peachgate Floor Coverings (Flooring); Hundter Douglas (Venetian Blinds); NSB Casements Ltd (Windows); Cliford Devlin Transport Ltd (Asbestos Removal); Becher Joinery (Joinery) Artwork in Boardroom: Nick Rodgers.

Simon Jersey
Accrington, UK

Architecture and Interior Design: Studio BAAD. Project Team: Philip Bintliff, Paul Lewis, Jim Loftus, Andy Nicholls, Ray Philips. Client: Simon Jersey. Main Contractor (Shell): Eric Wright Construction. Quantity Surveyor: Warrington Martin. Structural Engineer (Shell): Booth King Partnership. Structural Engineer (Glass Floors, Table and Stair): Dewhurst Macfarlane and Partners. Steelwork: Killelea. Cladding: Range Roofing. Glazing: Hayward Glass Systems. Sail Structure: Cooper Rigg. Sails: Landrell Fabric Engineering. Fit-out – Ceilings, Signage, Specialist Joinery and Furniture, Decoration, Electrics: Innerspace. Heating: R&D PC Rapid, MdKiernan Group. Heating Offices: Fishwick. Glass Floor, Table and Stair: Hayward Glass Systems. Table and Stair: Structural Stairways. Executive Furniture: Vitra.

Lowe and Partners/SMS
London, UK

Architecture and Interior Design: Sedley Place. Project Team: David Bristow, Mick Nash (Directors-in-Charge); Antonio Maduro, Matthias Felsch, Tim Hyman. Client: Sedley Place. Collaborating Architects: Charles Patten Architects. Project Team: Charles Patten, Bulend Medjid (Project Architect), Maureen Cornwell (Interior Designer). Cost Consultant: Boyden & Company. Architectural Service Engineer: Edwards & Zuck. Main Contractors: AJ Contracting; Ostreicher, Corporate Interiors Contracting. Limestone Floor: Stone Source; Minos Ltd. Lighting: Reggiani (Downlights), Windsor Workshop (Bespoke Lamps), Eddison Price (Boardroom Lighting), Artemide (Task Lamps), Ora (Uplights & Display Panels). Ceiling System: Steel Ceilings. Fitted Woodwork: Rimi Woodcraft. Reception Sofa and Chairs: Munrod Upholstery. Reception Desk, Boardroom Table, Office Tables, Bar Table Tops: Grongar Associates. Office Tables: Haford Furniture. Bar Seating: Catalytico. Aluminium Wall Sections: Cego Aluminium. Marquetry Screen: David Linely Co. Office Seating: Vitra (UK) Ltd. Stair Structure: Edelman Metalwork. Stained Glass Panels: Brian Clarke. Stained Glass Light Box and Stair Well Lighting: Mark Kruger Designs Light. Audio Visual System: Audio Visual Designs. Carpets: Brintons Carpets. Fluted Blocks in Simulated Ceramic: Amanda Sutton. Bronze and Glass Ceiling Light Fixtures in Bar: Marshall Howard.

LVA 2000
Lubeck, Germany

Architecture and Interior Design: Behnisch, Behnisch & Partner.
Project Team: Gunnar Ramsfjell (Project Leader), Martin Arvidson, Birger Bhandary, David Cook, Jorn Genkel, Martin Gremmel, Horst Muller, Martina Schaab, Jorg Usinger (Project Architects); Elke Altenburger, Thomas Balke, Marc Benz, Iris Bulla, Kathrin Dennig, Jutta Fritsch, Stefan Forrer, Pietro Granaiola, Heiko Krampe, Cecilia Perez, Matthias Schmidt, Timo Saller, Jan Soltau, Georg Taxhet, Karin Weigang. Collaborating Architect: Christian Kandzia. Client: State Insurance Agency. Project Management: Behnisch, Behnisch & Partner; Cronauer Beratung und Planung. Landscape Architect: WES & Partner. Stuctural Engineers: Weischede und Partner GmbH. Electrical Engineers: Planning Group KMO mbh. Mechanical Engineer: Rentschler & Riedesser. Building Physics: Engineering Office Langkau.

McDonald's, Milan
Italy

Architecture and Interior Design: Atelier Mendini.
Project Team: A. Mendini, F. Mendini, A. Balzari, G. Bertolini, B. Gregory, F. Rotella. Client: McDonald's Italia Company. Main Contractors: Freudenberg (Flooring); Crosara (Glass Wall); ICF (Offices and Furniture). Consultants: BMZ, Ing. Zambelli (A/C and Electrical Installation).

McDonald's Headquarters, Helsinki
Finland

Architecture and Interior Design: Heikkinen-Komonen Architects.
Project Team: Mikko Heikkinen, Markku Komonen, Janne Kentala (Project Architect), Hanna Euro, Antti Kononen, Markku Puumala, Sarlotta Narjus. Client: McDonald's Oy, JP Terasto Oy. Main Contractor: Skanska Etela-Suomi Oy. Landscape Architect: Gretel Hemgard. Construction Engineers: Projectus Team Oy. Geotechnical: Vesi-Hydro Oy. Façade: Teraselementti Oy. HEPAC: ABB Installaatiot Oy. Office Furniture: R. O. Loimulahti Oy.

Ministry of Defence
Abbey Wood, Bristol, UK

Architect and Masterplanning: Percy Thomas Partnership (Architects) Ltd.
Project Team: John Rudge (Masterplanner, Lead Architect), Clifford Martin, Ron Weeks, Robert Selley, Robert Mitchell, Richard Whitaker, Willie Harbinson, Russell Hones, Robert Firman, Andrew Nixon, Alaric Smith, Robert Parlane, Tim Burke, Richard Fisher, Steve Crosland-Mills, Tim Skudder, Mark Henerson, Christopher Warren, Neil Purkiss, Alsion Clifford-Smith, Heidi Harrison. Client: MOD. Space Planning and Interior Design: PTP Seward Ltd (Project Team: Julian Seward, Simon Jackson, Diana Monkhouse). Landscape: PTP Landscape & Urban Design Ltd. Project Team: Jane Findlay, Phil Champion, Chris Evans, Richard Sumner. Environmental Engineer: Hoare Lea & Partners. Structural/Civil Engineer: Ernest Green Partnership. Cost Consultants: Bucknall Austin Plc. Project Manager: Symonds Group. A-V Design: Acoustic Dimensions. Ecology: Bristol Ecological Consultants. Signage: Timothy Guy Associates.

Mission
London, UK

Architect and Interior Design: Misha Stefan. In-house building team. Eames Chairs.

Monsanto
St Louis, USA

Architecture and Interior Design: Holey Associates.
Project Team: John Holey, Julie Dwyer-Gower, Lori Pachelli, Edie Chaska, Greg Keffer, Paul Dent, Patrick Booth, Andra Martens, Bryant G. Rice, Jim Counts, Hal Tangen. Client: Monsanto Executive Committee. Development Consultant: UniDev LLC. Architect of Record: Hellmuth, Obata & Kassabaum Inc. MEO Engineer: Flack and Kurtz. Construction Manager: DM Jones Company. Energy Consultant: William McDonough & Partners; ENSAR Group Inc. Lighting Consultant: Clanton Engineering Inc. Schematic Lighting Consultant: Auerbach and Glasow. Furniture Systems Manufacturer: Herman Miller Inc. Furniture Management: Furniture Management Services Group. Carpets: Bentley. Terrazzo: American Terrazzo Company. Furniture Suppliers: Davis, Ted Boerner Furniture Design, Directions, R.A.G.E. through Millennium Collection, Metro Furniture, Azcast Products, Ycami, Vitra, Vecta, Design American. Lighting: Neo Ray, Steelcase Details, Columbia.

Nokia House
Espoo, Finland

Architecture and Interior Design: Helin & Siitonen Architects.
Project Team: Pekka Helin (Partner-in-Charge); Erkki Karonen (Project Architect); Harri Koski (Project Architect); Seija Ekholm, Jutta Haarti-Katajainen, Totti Helin, Mariitta Helineva, Tarja Hilden, Anne Jylha, Virpi Karonen, Antti Laiho, Kaarina Livola, Titta Lumio, Pertti Ojamies, Kirsi Pajunen, Katariina Takala, Sanna-Maria Takala. Client: Oy Nokia ab. Construction: Oy Matti Ollila & Co. Engineers. Electrical Engineers: Oy Tauno Nissinen Engineers. Heating and Ventilation: LVI-Niemi, Kari Helander Engineers. Interior Design: Iris Ulin; Kari Uusi-Heimala, Yrjo Wegelius (Interior Architect). Kitchen Design: Amica'Aino Heikkila. Landscape Architect: M-L Rosenbrjpjer Landscaping. Acoustics: Alpo Halme Architects. Lighting Suppliers: Erco, Bega, iGuzzini, Arteluce, Elektro-Valo, Ensto, Idman. Suppliers of Fixtures and Timberwork: Raision Puusepat, Vatialan Pussepat, Haapaveden Puukaluste, Kurikan Interioori, Oy Litorina Ab. Kitchen Appliances: Hackman Metos Oy. Furniture: Artek, Aptero, Avarte, Inno, Vivero, Mobel.

Natuzzi Americas Headquarters
High Point, North Carolina, USA

Architecture and Interior Design: Mario Bellini Associati Srl.
Project Team: Mario Bellini, Giovanna Bonfanti, Giovanni Cappelletti, Luigi Morellato (model). Client: Natuzzi. Main Contractor and Director of Works: Weaver Construction. Executive Architect: J. Hyatt Hammond Associates Inc. Structural

Engineer: Laurene and Rickher PC. Glazing Wall, Catwalks and Interior Windows: Nordisa Srl. Curved Wall, Metal Structures, Entrance Doors and Windows: Astec Srl.

Office-Daiwa
Tsuyama, Okayama Prefecture, Japan

Architecture and Interior Design: Toru Murakami Architect & Associates.
Client: Daiwa. General Contractor: Washida Construction. Structural Engineers: S.A.P. Architectural Structure. Mechanical Engineers: Mechanical Engineers AWAK; Moriki Mechanical Engineers.

Owens Corning World Headquarters
Toledo, USA

Architecture: Cesar Pelli & Associates.
Project Team: Cesar Pelli (Design Principal); Fred W. Clarke (Project Principal); Mark Shoemaker (Design Team Leader); Phillip Bernstein (Project Manager); Mihaly Turbucz, David Chen, Axel Zemborain, Julann Meyers, David Coon, Anne Haynes, Jane Twombly, Karen Koenig, William Traill. Client: Owens Corning. Architect of Record: Kendall/Heaton Associates, Inc. Interior Design: Harley Ellington Design; Steelcase Inc. Construction Organization: Hines Interests Limited Partnership. Engineers: CBM Engineers Inc. (Structural); Cosentini Associates (MEP); Avca Corporation (Civil). Landscape Architect: Balmori Associates. Acoustics: Cerami & Associates Inc. Curtainwall: Heitman & Associates. Artists: Architectural and Sculptural Glass – Thomas Patti.

Pomegranit
San Francisco, USA

Architecture and Interior Design: Holey Associates.
Project Team: John Holey, Carl Bridgers, Joan Diengorr, Edie Chaska, David Seidel, Greg Keffer. Client: Pomegranit. General Contractor: Plant Construction Company. Light Fixtures: Juno Lighting Inc. Carpets: Fortune Contract; Bigelow Carpets. Plasterwork: Tony Olea. Paint: ICI. Steelwork: Howard Wire Cloth Company. Furniture: Ken Gwin (Reception Desk); Herman Miller (Aeron Chair in Reception Area); Herman Miller (Eames Plywood Lounge Chair in Reception).

Prospect Pictures
London, UK

Architecture: Buschow Henley.
Client: Prospect Pictures. Main Contractor: Barlow Shopfitting. Structural Engineering: Dewhurst MacFarland. Acoustic Engineer: Alan

Saunders Associates. Suppliers: Filon (Fibreglass Partitions/Luminaires); Pietro Lara (Portuguese Limestone Floors), Vorwerk (Carpets), Encapsulite (Colour Gelled Fluorescent Lights); Barrie Cassey (Acoustic Studio Locks), Dryad (Shear Locks), Dorma (Floor Springs), Formica (Laminates), IKEA (Cabinets).

Rover Design and Engineering Centre
Gaydon, Warwickshire, UK

Architecture: Weedon Partnership.
Project Team: Terry Lee (Partner-in-Charge); John Carter (Associate and Project Architect), Philip Cole, Andy Griffiths, Tim Bennett, Gill Hammond. Client: Rover Group. Interior Designer: Monteith Scott Architectural Interiors with Weedon Partnership. Quantity Surveyor: Yeoman & Edwards. Structural Engineer: David J. Rolton Consulting Engineers. Services Engineer: Rolton Services Consultants. Landscape Architecture: Barry Chinn Associates. Acoustics: Applied Acoustic Design. Electrical Subcontractor: IDS Electrical. Mechanical Subcontractor: Briggs and Forrester. Structural Steelwork: Condor Structures. Light Fittings Manufacturer and Consultant: Thorn Lighting. Specialist Joinery: Worrall Joinery. Steel Staircase: Kingston Engineering. Internal Polished Blockwork (in street): Lignacite. Slate Flooring: Midland Marble. Reception Desk: Gordon Russell.

M&C Saatchi
London, UK

Architecture and Interior Design: Harper Mackay. Client: Scottish Provident/M&C Saatchi. Main Contractor: Morgan Lovell London Ltd. Project Manager: Cyril Leonard & Co. Service Engineers: Rybka Battle. Structural Engineers: Battle McCarthy. Furniture System: Viaduct.

Seghers Engineering
Klein Willebroek, Belgium

Architecture and Interior Design: Samyn and Partners.
Project Team: Ph. Samyn, J. Daels, K. de Mulder, N. Mulder, N. Milo, Ph van Caenegem, N. Vandendriessche, J. van Rompaey. Client: Seghers Engineering sa. Main Contractor: Van Poppel sa. Structural Design, Electrical and Plumbing Services: Seghers Engineering 'Water'; J. Meijersprl. Mechanical Services and HVAC: V.I.B. sprl. Acoustics: Katholieke Universiteit Leuven. Metal Structure and Glass Roof: Alu-Decor sprl. Glazed Partitions: Boermans Glas sa; Glascentrale Bavikhove sa; Jos Heylen. Spiral Staircase: Laeremans sa. Heating: O.F.F. sa. Electricity: Electro Industrieel sa.

Architecture and Interior Design: Apicella Associates.
Project Team: Lorenzo Apicella, Hilary Clark, Matthew Foster. Client: Coley Porter Bell. Main Contractor: Barlow Retail Ltd. Furniture Suppliers: Atrium, Vitra, Wilkahn. Carpet: Interface. Lighting: Artemide.

WMA Consulting Engineer
Chicago, USA

Architecture and Interior Design: Valerio Dewalt Train.
Project Team: Joseph M. Valerio (Principal-in-Charge/Design Principal); Neil Sheehan (Project Architect); Kasia Gawlik, Erica Pagel, Jason Hall, Marius Ronnett, Andrew To. Client: WMA Consulting Engineer. General Contractor: The Kaiser Loftrium. Mechanical/Electrical Engineering: WMA Mechanical Group. HVAC Ornamental Metals: Hill Mechanical Group. Millwork: Mellow Millwork. Flooring: Desks, Inc.

Yapi Kredi Bank
Gebze, Turkey

Architecture: John McAslan & Partners.
Project Team: John McAslan, Hiro Aso, Adrian Friend, Nick Eldridge, Andrew Potter, Judith Quartson, Piers Smerin, Jamie Troughton, Raj Rooperai, Roger Wu. Client: Yapi Kredi Bank. Associate Architect: Metex Istanbul. Project Management: Ove Arup & Partners. Façade Engineering: Arup Façade Engineering. Tensile Fabrics: Koch Hightex GmbH. Landscape Architect: Peter Walker.

INDEX OF ARCHITECTS, DESIGNERS AND PROJECTS